Your
Young Child
and You

Your
Young Child
and You

How to Manage
Growing-up Problems in the Years
from One to Five
by
ELEANOR WEISBERGER

Foreword by Dr. Benjamin M. Spock

A SUNRISE BOOK
E. P. DUTTON & CO., INC. NEW YORK 1975

Dutton-Sunrise, Inc., a subsidiary
of E. P. Dutton & Co., Inc.

LIBRARY OF CONGRESS CATALOGING IN PUBLICATION DATA

Weisberger, Eleanor.
Your young child and you.

"A Sunrise book."
1. Children—Management. 2. Child study. I. Title.
HQ769.W43   1975   649'.12'3   75–5988

Published simultaneously in Canada by Clarke, Irwin & Company
Limited, Toronto and Vancouver
ISBN: 0–87690–171–2

For Susan, Betsy, and Debby
in memory of Austin

Acknowledgments

To Case Western Reserve University Medical School, the host that permitted my advanced training in Child Psychoanalysis and to Dr. Any Katan who led the program, I owe a therapist's fundamental debt.

To Dr. Douglas Bond, former Chief of the Department of Psychiatry, to Dr. John Flumerfelt and Dr. Willard Boaz, also of that department, I am particularly grateful because of their enthusiasm and support.

To the Child Psychiatry Clinic at Hanna Pavilion, I am indebted for the twenty years of exposure to the education and supervision of outstanding clinicians in the field of child psychiatry and social work.

So many people have contributed to the views expressed in the book, I would not know where to begin to make acknowledgment. However, I want to specifically thank teachers in the program of the Cleveland Center for Research in Child Development. Among the many who were closest to my work were Miss Marian Barnes, Miss Elizabeth Daunton and Dr. Jane Kessler. However, none of them can be held responsible for the form the book has taken. The application of a holistic theory of child development to child-rearing practice may derive from my training, but I alone must be responsible for the book's content. This is genuinely a case where the sponsors are not to be held responsible for the views expressed by the writer.

For support in the editorial work, I would like to express particular thanks to Miss Lisa Drew, Mrs. Barbara Feldman, Mrs. Susan Gordon (a colleague, a daughter, as well as an editor), and Miss Wendy Weil.

For help in the typing, I am indebted to Miss Jan Harrity and Mrs. Shirley Teplitsky who bore the many changes involved in the writing with patience and good cheer.

Contents

Foreword

Elly Weisberger and I got to know each other while I was on the faculty of Case Western Reserve University Medical School, where she still is working. I was teaching child development and doctor-patient relationships to medical students and she was a child therapist and parent counselor in the children's clinic. Whenever I attended a child psychiatry conference at which she discussed a family's problem, I was impressed by two things: her sympathetic understanding of both the child's and the parents' difficulties (some therapists tend to be either pro-child or pro-parent), and the way she could present the problem in clear, sensible, human terms—without jargon.

When I came to organize a course in child development and child management for undergraduate students, I asked Elly Weisberger to teach it with me, which she did for a number of years—in the same clear, sensible, human way. (It proved a popular course, with three hundred students.)

In this book for parents, Elly Weisberger explains how they can communicate with their children about some of the commonest problems of the first five years of life—toilet training, everyday management and discipline, jealousy, sex education, going-to-bed fears, children's anxieties over parents' absences for vacations and emergencies, reactions to the death of a relative or neighbor, preparing a child for hospitalization.

She tells how small children feel about these situations—including their surprising misunderstandings—and how parents can explain the realities and requirements in a way that gains their children's cooperation.

She is particularly helpful in showing parents how to point out to children their negative feelings—of anger and fear—which are the ones that cause the most tension in family life and that block children's progress toward maturity. All through the book she quotes children's poignant or grumpy remarks and gives practical, no-nonsense replies that a parent could use almost word for word.

In earlier generations, when children showed fear—as of a coming tonsillectomy—they were often misled or else urged to behave and deny their fears. When they'd reveal the slightest hostility toward a parent, brother, or sister, they were shamed into repressing it. (That's what always happened to me.) As a result, many tensions persisted. Now we have learned how much better people function—and get along with each other—if they are allowed to have their feelings and can talk about them.

But it's hard for parents brought up under the old philosophy to recognize feelings—of their children or of themselves—and to discuss them comfortably. That's just where Elly Weisberger's book fits in. It makes a valuable companion piece for *Baby and Child Care*. I wish I had been able to write it myself.

Benjamin M. Spock, M.D.

Introduction

Mothers and fathers today get a wealth of conflicting advice from pediatricians, books, magazines, and television. Nobody knows who to believe, but almost all parents look for answers at one time or another. Children are hard to raise, and the answers are not easily apparent by observing the children themselves.

I came to write this book after many years of working in a children's clinic as a child therapist. A mother myself, I began to recognize that many normal parents of normal children were confused by the various points of view they had been offered.

Meanwhile, from my experience in treating children I had learned a good deal about what was likely to go wrong. I thought I had learned enough from my training to say something about what could be done right. With this in mind, some years ago I started meeting with groups of interested mothers of children under five. I chose this particular age group because I felt the most significant development takes place in the early years. The groups were open to all mothers who were interested. Several hundred have now passed through these informal weekly sessions. It was they who pressed me to write this book.

Actually, not everyone said, "Why don't you write it down?" What they did do was press me to answer specific questions about *their* specific children; and they did not let me generalize—at least not for very long. This book, then, is really their book. If it should prove to have value for you, it is because it reflects their realism and candor. Every story in it is theirs.

What I learned very early from these discussions was that everyone faced problems in child rearing. As the years went on, I began to see how little parents knew about normal child development. This gap in knowledge occurred in mothers who had read a lot and in mothers who had read little or not at all. Clearly something was wrong if so many burdened themselves with constant self-criticism. An underlying theme was heard again and again. "If I were handling my child better, this would not be happening." The mothers had an almost overwhelming sense of responsibility for their children's behavior and seemed not to know when, if ever, the children should be held accountable. It was as if they were on trial in the public press. Other households, they felt, were better run, more serene, more tranquil, and only they suffered from suppertime squabbles, messy pants, sibling rivalry, and big mouths. They had been led to expect that children evoke the best in us. The fact that they also evoke the worst in us was apparently the best-kept secret in the United States.

I became aware that many of today's parents were paying a price for their greater sophistication about child development. Since these parents knew the early years were important to their children's future mental stability, they were often unable to *act* for fear of making a mistake. Other generations of parents, if often misguided, had been sure of themselves. They exuded authority with a capital A. And if their children experienced emotional mixups in their adult years, these parents did not feel they were responsible. This does not mean that the old way was better. But it does mean it was easier. How nice for parents that children were to be seen and not heard. How gratifying that children were makers of their own destiny.

The mothers I saw in the groups operated under assumptions they presumed to be scientific. Many seemed to share what I came to label the Understanding Fallacy; that is, if a child has a reason to act in a certain way and psychology explains his right to that reason, then parents are to be *understanding* (or, as interpreted by my mothers, *tolerant*). What defied comprehension was that their children often seemed to behave worse when faced with understanding and patience. The "A reason is an excuse" phenomenon seemed to rest heavily on conscientious mothers. Psychological insights that should have helped parents manage better had somehow been distorted to mean little or no management. Somehow their increased understanding of the child's world had become a license for unacceptable behavior. A favorite theme, "This too will pass," had often left parents waiting indefinitely.

The truth is that the infant starts out in the world wanting what he wants when he wants it. Parents are the child's first educators, and it is they who have to support a more mature level of functioning. Conflict, therefore, is inevitable. It is a child's coming to terms with conflict in himself that aids maturity. While some children seem to have an easier time accepting life's demands than others (infants are different in their responses right from the cradle), there is little question that all would prefer to have things go their way. When you have to lead them your way the trouble starts. You want your child clean; he wants to be dirty. You want him polite; he likes foul language. I could go on. Earlier generations forced these issues, and we know now how this often engendered a phony compliance: superficial manners on the outside, anger and rebellion within.

This book is an attempt to help you guide your child in the direction you think best for him. It assumes you wish to raise a child to become a responsible, self-directed person. Knowledge of the child's inner developmental phases should help you be more effective in the civilizing process. You work *with* the child's grain rather than against it. Understanding the reasons for the recommendations given here should help you move in a direction that is compatible with your own lifestyle and yet constructive for your youngster. We want children to grow up, not just grow. We need to know not only what steps to take for them but how to manage ourselves during the process. Knowing what to expect ahead of time is useful. In effect, this book is about life as it is lived, not as a vision (motherhood with a capital M) or as a scientifically determined project.

The main focus is on the parents' role as educators of preschool children, not in the reading and writing sense, but in the sense of aiding the development of emotional maturity. The book is concerned with discipline (Latin root *disciplina,* meaning "teaching") in the broadest sense. The recognition that development is making changes within a child can help you select the issues which he will be able to manage successfully at various ages.

For this reason, I have begun with a chapter about toilet training. It is at toilet-training time that your role as educator leaps to the fore. Before that time you were largely responding to the baby's needs and rhythm. Whether your methods leaned more toward scheduling or more toward self-demand, you were primarily involved with your child's eating, elimination, and sleep. A physiological process was going on which demanded pretty concrete care from you. True, your child's mind was developing as you provided this fundamental nurturing, but beyond your pleasure in his progress you were not called upon actively to ensure his growth. Your care and love did that.

This does not mean that these earlier phases were easy. They may well have been difficult, depending on the child. But you could compensate for your lack of experience by seeking advice from your family doctor or pediatrician as well as from a number of excellent books available on the subject of infant care. (For example, weaning, which is in a sense the first "takeaway," is covered comprehensively in such books.) Because of these factors, I have chosen not to deal with the first year and a half of your youngster's life, except in passing. To do so would be to duplicate what is available from these other fine sources.

The recommendations I make for mothers in this book are meant to apply to fathers as well. Fathers are important to their children, and a concerted effort by both parents, when possible, is best. Mothers are featured prominently, however, because in the traditional family it is the mother who is the central caretaking figure for young children.

Throughout I have referred to the caretaking parent as "she" and the child as "he," simply because to do otherwise in English is impossibly awkward. In some families the father is more directly involved in child care, and the philosophy and techniques advocated here apply to him as well. The more involved a father is, the more he needs to know what a mother knows, so in families where the father acts as caretaker, read "father" for "mother." His unique position as father (see Chapter XII) is not lost because of this. The principles of child rearing given in the pages that follow apply to the caretakers of all young children—be they fathers, mothers, or parent substitutes.

Your
Young Child
and You

I
Toilet Training

"When my son leaves home, I expect he'll be clean," said one wistful mother to a friend about her lack of success in toilet training her three-year-old.

Another mother said impatiently, "I'm tired of putting on a variety show every time my little boy goes to the john. There has to be a better system."

Others, confused by conflicting advice, tend to press for cleanliness in fits and starts, try this technique and that, as they hear that one or another method has worked for someone else's child. Treats are given; stories are told; threats are made; sittings are forced. Frustrated parents may spank their toddler when he fails to respond to these efforts.

Mothers look on toilet training as a distasteful chore that has to be done *somehow, some time,* by *somebody.* Many hope it will happen all by itself, and there are just enough mothers who proclaim instant victory to put everyone else in a bind when their own efforts are not immediately successful. Everyone seems to heave a sigh of relief when cleanliness is finally achieved, but no one seems very clear about why or how it happened. One woman said, "It was a battle all the way." Another said, "I found I'd rather clean him up myself than face the mess."

Why should this normal step in our children's development provoke so much feeling on our part? Why should sensible parents approach training a young child with such distaste?

One explanation is that when you undertake toilet training you are asking your child to do something *your* way for the very first time. Outside of the weaning of the first year (which you do *to* him), you have asked very little of your child. For the most part you have been the giver, the helper, the good guy. You have been largely responding to his needs. Now the roles have shifted. You are asking something of him. This changes the helper-helpee relationship you have known since his birth, and it is possible that your unfamiliarity with what constitutes proper behavior under these changed circumstances makes you uncomfortable. In a way, you don't know how to ask, and your child doesn't know how to respond. It is the first time for both of you. After you have had a number of children, *you* may be more experienced, but your child isn't. It's still the first time for him. And he has a different personality from each of the others, so that once more it can feel like a brand-new experience for you as well.

There is a conflict hidden in this problem, although it may be difficult to sift out. Once you become an asker, a requester, a "Do it in the pot, please" person, the child acquires a power he never had before. He can say "no" very emphatically. As a matter of fact, a child tends to be in his most negative stage (a normal phase of growth) just about the time you decide to toilet-train. He seems to have only one word in his vocabulary and that word is "no." He behaves as though being asked to give means being asked to give in. So the issue of conflict has to be faced. Do you push in the face of this resistance? Some child-care experts advise you to stop toilet training and wait until he is more ready. But when is that? These are a few of the issues that seem to make a normal step for your child a source of discomfort for you.

WHAT TOILET TRAINING REALLY IS

Toilet training is not just for being clean. In a real sense it's not a training process at all. It is the first step the child takes in a learning experience that goes on for the rest of his life. It is his first move toward becoming responsible for what he does, and it sets a precedent for future learning. It is, then, really more of an educational process than anything else.

You should regard toilet training as part of the child's own evolution. Through the process of training, you help him take steps to be clean for *himself.* What goes on during the process is as important as the results you hope to achieve.

For the majority of children, this learning process takes time, often months. It is not an isolated aspect of growth. Your child gains self-control in many ways as you expect more and more of him over a period of time.

My recommendations work *with,* not against, the normal maturing of your child. You want him to be responsible for his own body functions for his own sake, and you would like to be free of smelly diapers for your own. The two wishes are not incompatible. Actually they work together. One of the first aims of toilet training is to help your child achieve independence. The more he does for himself, the less you are involved.

Every measure recommended in this chapter leads to help-ing your child master the process for himself. What you will be doing, in effect, is providing the props so that he can take over. But since a child is growing and changing all the time, a gradual increase in your expectations goes along with his ever-increasing abilities. That's why the idea of process is so important. At the same time that you help him to be respon-sible for himself, he is growing older and more mature. This means that you take new measures as you go along. You require more of him as he matures.

FIRST STEPS IN TOILET TRAINING

The steps that follow are designed to help you help your child achieve independence and mastery of his own body functions. There are three steps to begin with:

1. Buy a potty chair. These chamber pots with outhouse-type seats are best, since the child can reach the seat without your assistance. This saves you wear and tear and allows the child to assert his authority over his own territory. Some recommend small seat attachments to the big toilet, but young children have difficulty reaching the toilet and are often afraid they will fall in and be flushed away. However, if your child prefers to use the regular toilet, don't make an issue of it. Just be sure to have a seat attachment and a step stool nearby for him to climb on. The idea is to have him manage it alone.

2. Buy many, many pairs of training pants, perhaps a dozen to start. Buy the best pants available—ones that are tight enough to hold in unexpected accidents and yet loose enough so he can pull them up and down himself. "Best" does not necessarily mean most expensive, merely put together well enough so leakage is reduced. I'm also greatly in favor of boxer-type shorts and jeans with elastic tops, for both sexes. These too can be pulled up and down easily by the child. Zippers, suspenders, and buttons, which are fine for the older child, merely get in the way at this time. Here again, he's on his own.

3. Buy a sponge. You'll also need a bucket, but the old diaper pail will do nicely. You've been soaking his diapers in it for what feels like years. This will now be used for soaking the training pants, which are the diapers' successors. The sponge is for mopping up mistakes.

A BEGINNING TIMETABLE

The following timetable is flexible, but it does offer guidelines.

Sometime when your little one is between fifteen and eighteen months old you start to talk to him about body functions, using your family euphemisms, like "dudu" and "weewee" or "poop" and "tinkle." His vocabulary is limited at this point, so you will be doing most of the talking. Every family has its own endearing terms, and far be it from me to traumatize anyone into saying "BM" and "urinate." It doesn't matter what you call the functions, but it is important to name them as he performs them.

This is an introducing time. You have waited until he is able to stay dry for several hours at a time. He is walking independently. He has a few words and seems to catch on when you name things. So the physiological readiness which is necessary for training is starting to come. You leave him in diapers during this early phase.

Put the new potty in the bedroom or anywhere else that is convenient for you and visible to your child. At first, suggest to him that he sit on the potty seat with his diapers on. That's to get him used to it. Try to catch him occasionally to help him get the point. A grunt may alert you to imminent action. You can lead him to the chair, suggesting mildly, while unfastening safety pins, that this is the place to perform. You can say something like, "This is where you are to make dudu." You can add, "Big boys and big girls make it in here. When you are bigger you will do it in here too."

Perhaps twice a day you can make this trek to the potty with him. You don't want to overdo it. Tell him what he's to do there (or what he's already done, most likely), and that's about it for two or three months. Let him watch you empty the contents of his diaper into the potty so that he sees what goes where. It's preliminary and gradual, and it sets the stage. You continue to change him as you've done before.

At eighteen months or so, the real effort can begin. Before this age the muscles are generally not mature enough to operate with control. Why knock yourself out until you can expect some cooperation? Kids vary, of course, in their readiness for this, just as they vary in beginning to talk or walk, but somewhere in the second half of the second year they're usually ready. Be prepared for some balkiness occasionally, as a child is usually doing something else when he's eliminating. Often he resents the interruption, so try to choose the time for the trek with some tact. Don't be discouraged by lack of interest on his part. It's a venture that requires patience. There is a human tendency not to like change, and your asking something new of him brings normal resistance. That's why the preparatory education is helpful.

Try not to start the program while other changes are impending—for example, if Grandma is coming for Christmas or a new baby is expected. Toilet training takes effort, and it's hard to concentrate if there are many other changes cluttering up the scene. He is too busy adjusting to those. Also, when you yourself are overwhelmed with other things, it is hard to be patient.

You say there never is a right time? You have a point. The trick is to find a relatively unchaotic time to begin—some time that you deliberately eke out of a busy schedule. In a way, training your child demands the same kind of effort you would make to learn any new skill yourself.

Once you begin, prepare to stay with it. It will probably take three to six months to achieve the desired results. If there's illness or unexpected guests or other disruptions in routine that upset his progress, don't revert to diapers. Stay with the plan but allow for some adjustment. For example, if the child has a bout of diarrhea, put on two pairs of training pants and plastic pants as well. But don't reverse your stand on his giving up diapers. By not changing what you expect from him you show your confidence in his ability to get back into the swing when the illness is over. Continue as before, recognizing that although he won't do as well for a while, this is only a temporary setback. Pick up where you left off and keep going. The worst that can happen is that the training may take a bit longer.

The idea that the child is a genuine participant in the

training process is a new one to most parents. So be patient if others criticize your approach. When you see toilet training as an educational process that affects your child's total development, you will feel that the extra trouble and effort are worthwhile.

NEXT STEPS IN TOILET TRAINING

1. Place the potty chair in the bathroom. If there isn't a bathroom on the first floor, put the potty chair somewhere where he can get to it easily. A hall or corner of the kitchen may not be too esthetic, but it has its merits in that, at the ages of one and a half to two, toddlers tend to stray a little but always come back to where Mommy is.

2. One day, announce the following: "You are getting to be a big boy (or girl) now, and so Mommy bought you these new training pants." You show him the pile of training pants in the bathroom or wherever the potty chair is located. He is bound to be intrigued. The quantity alone will dazzle him.

Don't worry if he's not talking much. At eighteen months he is comprehending more than you know, because a great deal of understanding precedes speech. You continue: "And so I'm putting your diapers away—because you can now wear big boy (or girl) pants and do your dudu and wee-wee in the potty chair all by yourself." You demonstrate by putting the diapers away in a closet or on a high shelf. Look pleasantly authoritative or at least moderately expectant but not beseeching. Don't let him get the feeling you care too much. If he ever gets that idea, he can bedevil you when he's angry. Then point to the potty chair and say, "Do it here." And, "This is where big boys and girls do it." Show him how easy the new pants are to slip up and down.

Generally he will smile benignly, delightedly step into the new pants, and promptly wet into his socks. Sneakers are a boon during this irritating phase.

3. Put away his plastic or rubber pants. This may sound

destructive, particularly if you are devoted to your carpeting, but there's a sound reason for it. If his training pants are cozily tucked inside his rubber pants, as his diapers used to be, he doesn't know what's happening. He's not sure if he's done something or not. Without plastic or rubber pants, his attention is drawn to the sogginess and/or smelliness of his training pants and he knows that something has happened. It is upon this gradual awareness that you begin to capitalize. You can save a few pair to be used at nap and bedtime since training at those times comes later.

In the baby days before training pants, he was quite content to stay in his messes and passively acquiesce to your changing him. The situation is now altered as he begins to feel the consequences of what he has done. The new discomfort, of which he gradually becomes aware, is a factor in his learning. Some children seem not to mind the mess and that can upset you. But if you stick with this method, you will find that eventually the mess is a constructive teacher. For the time being you are allowing him to suffer the consequences of wetting and soiling.

Unfortunately, you too will be experiencing the consequences. I admit it takes courage to let Junior soak into whatever he's standing on. You are a homemaker as well as a mother, and if you have worked hard to get that handsome carpet in your house, it may seem quite absurd to encourage your toddler to spoil it. But any permanent damage can be prevented. Baking soda or salt, when sprinkled over the offending spot, makes both stain and odor disappear. For new carpet owners who may be even more fastidious, a mixture of one quart of warm water to two tablespoons of white vinegar and two tablespoons of detergent makes an effective spot remover. Keep a bottle of the solution made up in the kitchen; this may help you deal more calmly with the results of a messy bottom and the owner of same. Club soda has proved useful in this connection too. It works well on both stain and odor. One mother recommends scotch and soda. The scotch is for you and the soda is for the spot.

The reason I am so explicit about how you handle the messiness is that it is essential to allow your child to take this step. By your not being overly concerned about accidents in the beginning, you start a process where he becomes the one to be concerned, not you. You are not vulnerable to the emotional threat of a dirty upset. You are able to keep your poise in the face of the possibility of messing.

4. It's a step in the right direction when he starts using the proper word for the appropriate function. Unfortunately, this may be *after* the fact. "Dudu!" he will shout ecstatically as he runs around the house alerting Daddy, and any other captive listener, to this marvelous accomplishment. Sometimes when he is more verbal he says, "Dudu, potty," indicating he knows where it is supposed to go. This doesn't mean he is doing it in the right place. Still, some connections are being made. He is making some inferences for himself.

After several weeks of this you begin to say to Junior, "Next time, tell me *before* you make dudu." When you hear a grunt or recognize a pre-pee-pee expression, say matter of factly, "I think you have to go to the potty now." Lead him to it and help him take his pants off, if he doesn't resist you —but then leave. Pray silently if you wish, but that is all.

5. Don't cajole him, or read him stories, or tell him he'll get a treat if he performs. That removes his responsibility from the action. He then performs for the treat, rather than because it's a job that must be done.

Do tell him he's doing it right when he does, but refrain from praising him extravagantly. After all, it's not *really* an uncommon accomplishment.

You can say something like, "What a big boy you are! How pleased you must be with yourself." This is a sneaky point. It tells him he is to be congratulated for what *he* has done. It praises him for *his* success in doing a "big boy" thing. It isn't saying, "Please, pretty please, do this for me."

Now, all of us mothers *feel* they should perform for us. If our thoughts could be written over our heads as in little comic-strip clouds, they would be saying, "Please, please, dear child, do it for me." And, "I am sick to death of all this mopping up."

Or, "I am tired of chasing wiggly, stubborn, uncooperative toddlers who keep saying 'no' to everything."

And, "Whatever happened to that darling baby who was so sweet and adorable?"

Or, "Certainly he can't be teething at *this* age!"

At nineteen, twenty, or even twenty-four months of age he seems to understand what you mean, but he doesn't seem to be cooperating, despite your educational efforts. As he soils your rug or wets the newly washed kitchen floor, smiling beatifically at you and the mess he has created, you may begin to feel a strange dislike for this once-loved child. This is the time for positive action.

6. Give him the sponge. Tell him he must clean up his mess. An important concept is demonstrated here. It is the idea of consequence following act. You let a normal function occur with the idea that he will slowly see the connection between what he did and the undoing of same. He is being allowed to be responsible for himself.

He is a toddler and no longer a baby. He may still look like a baby to you because you are with him daily and can't see the changes in a dramatic way. But he is ready for more responsibility as each month passes.

The cleaning up may not be so clean; you may want to do it over yourself—but wait until he's in bed. For the time being you can say, "Billy made the mess. Billy clean it up!" You can add, if you're still coherent, "Next time Billy does it in the potty like a big boy."

In the cleanup demonstration you calmly show him how to:

a. Rinse his pants in the toilet. (A wire brush is useful here.)
b. Soak the pants in the diaper pail.
c. Pick up any assorted leavings with a tissue.
d. Wash the spot with a sponge.

After the first or second delighted sloshing in the john, he will find this pretty onerous. No child I ever knew enjoyed cleanups after the first few weeks. When he can't go outside without clean pants, he'll make some connections for himself. The idea of consequence following act is built right in.

Sometimes battle lines are drawn. You say, "Do it!" He says, "No!" You say, "Potty." He soils his pants. Try to avoid the battle by choosing your own good time for a confrontation. When the lady outside is honking her horn and Junior has to be ready, you can't very well make his cleaning up a major issue. He can refuse and you are pressed into doing it for him. Plan ahead for a confrontation in which you can't be blackmailed. For example, a trip to a friend's house can be canceled if your child doesn't clean himself up before you go. Usually, one or two of these planned-ahead confrontations are enough to get the point across. You cannot force him to clean up, but you can build in some negative consequences for him if he refuses.

It takes time after you start him on cleanups; it may take months. What makes it worthwhile is his slowly dawning awareness that he is responsible for what he has done.

As one little girl said, "It's my job." When a child masters cleaning up, he is very proud. His self-esteem is very great, and it is his victory, not yours. How much sweeter for him! Often, after success is achieved, the "tricycle syndrome" may be observed. Body control in one area gives him the boost he needs to try in others. He mounts his bike and shouts with glee, "Look, Mommy! No hands!" His pride in his ability to control his body functions gives him the confidence to be more venturesome about other skills. The cleanliness achievement is only part of his success. The mastery of self is the greater gain.

7. After a time, allow him to take the step of emptying the contents of the potty into the toilet. He may prefer to delay this for a while and he may not want you to flush the contents away immediately. Again, the child's immature thinking

that this "into the pot" business is a great accomplishment can have you delay flushing for a time. First he hears "Oh, how grown up you are!" Then he sees "Whoosh!" That these productions of his need not really be saved takes a bit of comprehending. When he is used to going by himself, he can be asked to empty the pot himself.

A GENERAL TIMETABLE

You can visualize the actual training as being done in three stages. First, you tell him what he's supposed to do and show him where to do it. Second, you acknowledge with him what happened. Finally, you let him be responsible for the results. If you've started training pants at about eighteen months, you should be ready to have him do his own cleanups about a month or two later (depending on your ability to give the matter your full attention).

Children vary a bit in readiness, but here is a general guide:

Fifteen to eighteen months	Introducing time. Name functions, lead him to potty chair, sit him on chair with diapers on. Next, remove diapers and sit him on chair. You still do the cleaning up.
Eighteen months	Training pants and potty chair. The phrase, after a month of messing, is "Next time, tell me before."
Twenty to twenty-two months	You expect him to clean up. You show him how to clean up as well as how to wipe himself, even though in most instances you have to give some assistance in both.

After you take the plunge, try not to go back to diapers, even though the temptation is there. Back and forth is too confusing for him. Once you begin, you go for broke. Your determination on this basis is very telling. He knows you are serious, and he feels more secure about his chances of succeeding.

If by chance you have let things slide and your child is three and a half and you're still waiting for a sign from him that he's ready, don't wait. Start. You have to take the initiative. Don't be dissuaded by teasing, orneriness, and evasion —the usual lifestyle of toddlers.

Your toddler can say stubbornly, "I won't," as one little boy I know did, adding to his mother's chagrin, "It's the Mommy's job." He can say it, of course, but don't you be the patsy and follow his advice. It's not good for him and it certainly isn't good for you.

How do you get a twenty-two-month-old to clean up? You are not really expecting a cleanup job; you are expecting participation in *his* cleaning up *his* mess. You *can* help him. It's not that hard once you get over thinking of your child as a baby. You will recognize that he can do it when you make your expectations clear. He understands more than he says and he is taking a lot of his cues from you. He will respond to the consistent expectation of your tone.

Often mothers of boys delay training because they have been told boys are slower in this connection. I'm not sure if there is any real evidence to support this, but I do know that a mother's resolve is sapped if she doesn't believe in the child's capability. An expectant attitude is better for both sexes, and I would expect as much of a boy as I do of a girl. A confident attitude on your part helps a lot, for children pick up indecisiveness. What works is the fact that every time he makes a mistake, he has to face up to it. Learning proceeds, if in a zigzag fashion, when you allow this to happen.

LATER STEPS IN TOILET TRAINING

Bowel control may precede bladder control, although children vary in this regard. The point is not to count successes on a daily basis but rather to feel the child is moving in the right direction over a period of time. He is drier this week than last or this month than last, for example. Some children may attain bladder control at night as well as bowel control. But I would go slowly regarding naptime or night training. Keep plastic pants over training pants at naptime and bedtime and don't expect him to stay dry at those times. You can't ask him to do too many things at once.

Once he has mastered day training fairly completely, and you see occasional dryness at night, you can begin to let him take responsibility for night wetting. Tell him this is the grownup way. Remove the plastic pants and announce that he can get up to go to the bathroom. You can say, "You are managing the potty during the day like a grownup boy. Now you can do this at naptime and bedtime." Let him know that he is allowed to get out of bed if he needs to. Leave the sides of the crib down or move the child to a junior bed where he can hop in and out. If you have space, keep both beds in his room so he has a choice for a while. It makes the bed change more gradual.

Ask him if he would like a night light to help get him to his destination. You can suggest a flashlight, which might be fun for him.

Another alternative is to put the potty in the bedroom— if you don't mind having it there at night. He can empty it in the morning.

Choose which aids work best for your child. Tell him about these proposals ahead of time so that he sees their connection with staying dry. In fact, every time you take a step with him, be sure to tell him what you're doing. Even if you're not sure he comprehends it, tell him anyhow.

Sometimes wetting or soiling at naptime and bedtime is a

way of evading toilet training. If so, discuss it with him. "You're not supposed to do this in bed; you're supposed to do it in the potty." If he persists, stick to your expectations. He must change his own bedding if he soils or wets while asleep. Between three and four a child can be asked to soak his sheets. After four he can put them in the washer.

Here again it's his own doing.

This is only partially true, of course. You stack the cards by having him feel the discomfort of his mistakes. But at least he is presented squarely with some of the choices available to him. If he prefers messiness for a while, this is okay too. Young children normally go through a stage of enjoying messes. You can stand it if you know it's a temporary phase. The learning for him comes in having to do his own cleaning up.

Sometimes children play with their stools. This is a misconception of what stools are, and you have to correct it. If he starts to mess in this fashion tell him "no." Get him some clay. Tell him in true Haim Ginott fashion that "clay is for playing—BMs are for the toilet." Cleanups should be encouraged by you but done by him. Don't be too concerned if he's not too neat in the beginning. He'll improve as he gets older. An assist from you is all right, but try to be less and less involved as times goes on.

Don't be concerned with how long it takes. The date of your child's success is far less important than the process by which he learns to achieve it. In fact, it is the process of coming to terms with cleanliness that makes this method so valuable. This should help you withstand criticism from mothers who claim more rapid success. This method actually benefits from time. Many children complete day training by age two or two and a half; others take longer. Night training often is not accomplished until between the ages of three and four. In fact, occasional accidents continue to occur up to the age of five at various times of stress, even during the day.

Your son may prefer to stand up to urinate. Some mothers

use a piece of toilet paper in the potty as a target to aid him in directing his stream. That's fine, but don't worry about it or press for it. Deflectors on the potty take care of this problem in the beginning if he is willing to sit down to urinate. However, if the deflector is so unwieldy or sharp that it is an obstacle, remove it and encourage him to direct his stream downward. "I hold it like a pencil," said two-and-a-half-year-old Mark. Later, when he shows interest he can be encouraged to perform standing up.

EMOTIONS AND TRAINING

Psychologically, the toilet trainee is going through a period of conflicting desires. On the one hand, he loves you dearly and very much wants to please you. I don't want to dwell on this because an oversolicitous mother can come to feel that the child is demonstrating his love for her when he performs properly. You want to allow it to be his business, which in the most basic sense it is. Yet, in the background, his love for you does play a part. That is why your positive expectation counts more with him than anyone else's. You carry a weight you don't even know you have.

The other side of the coin is that he is now his own person. From a passive, compliant, and cuddly baby he has become a mass of resistance and "nos." Suddenly, when you try to diaper him, he arches his back with leonine menace, bouncing all over the bed to escape you.

The pattern of complying sometimes and refusing other times reflects an inner struggle that has nothing to do with you. He is learning some things for himself, and he has weighty questions to answer.

Yes?
No?
Will I?
Won't I?
Here?

There?

Now?

Later?

Don't be afraid of his anger, which will pop out from time to time. Anger is a normal emotion and a young child can feel it as much as anyone else. There will be moments when he gets pretty mad about having to clean up. It is human nature to prefer that someone else do the dirty work. Your firmness about its being his job, no matter how upset he is, helps support his growing character development. We all have to do things in life we don't want to do.

One two-year-old cleaned up her BM mess agreeably enough, but then crayoned the bathroom wall with her mother's best lipstick. Her mother went into the bedroom to cool down. (Fifteen minutes were required to prevent infanticide.) She then said to Ellen, "You made a mess because I had you clean up your BM mess. Now you must clean up this one too." (Lighter fluid is great on crayons and lipstick, though the child should use it under supervision of course.) She and Ellen cleaned the wall together.

She then used a story to help Ellen understand her "I won't" feelings. (See Chapter VII on the use of the story.) She told her daughter that sometimes Ellen didn't want to clean up and sometimes she did. Sometimes Ellen wanted to be a big girl and play with toys and visit friends. But sometimes she wanted to be a baby and have Mommy clean up for her, like Mommy used to do when Ellen was a tiny baby.

The story acknowledged the child's conflicting desires—the wish to be more grown up and take a progressive step and the wish to have things the way they used to be. Her mother remained firm in her expectation and did not let up on the request. She did acknowledge Ellen's contrary feelings. Knowing that her mother understood helped Ellen to continue the training. Understanding does not mean yielding, however.

While anger is a normal human feeling, the two-year-old

seems particularly prone to give vent to it. It's as if this particular emotion is somehow connected with his growing independence. Don't retreat in the face of it. It is not good for children to avoid responsibility by bullying. The fact was, it was Ellen's job. The feeling was, she didn't want to do it. The final outcome—she did it. The ultimate feeling—she liked herself better for doing well.

Those who promote a casual, laissez-faire approach to child rearing often forget the value of pride in achievement. Allowing children to *feel* negative emotions doesn't mean that we let them off the hook in terms of expectation. But living up to expectations takes time. Once you realize this, it's easier to be patient. The struggle the child is undergoing is important education for him.

A WORD ABOUT ENEMAS

It is important to avoid enemas and suppositories. To a child, an enema is an overwhelming assault. Perhaps a story will illustrate what I mean.

A four-year-old girl was given an enema and a severe withholding problem ensued. She withheld her BMs for two weeks at a time. It took many weeks of talk on the mother's part to undo the distress and anger of this child before she was able to resume natural functioning. Trying to feel less responsible, the mother told the child that Dr. Green had recommended the enema, which was indeed the case. A year later this little girl asked her mother in a conversational tone, "Oh, by the way, did they ever let Dr. Green out of jail?" That's what she thought enema givers deserved!

Make clear to your doctor that you are opposed to anal manipulation as a way of helping bowel function. Most doctors will agree to the use of oral stool softeners or extra fruit. After all, what goes in must come out. Recognizing that fact may make you less tense about your child's performance. Some children perform daily; others have only one or two BMs a week.

Another word about this sensitive area. Rectal thermometers can be frightening to children. Oral or underarm temperature taking does away with a lot of unnecessary anxiety. Many hospitals have already recognized this and no longer use rectal thermometers.

Again, I urge you to recognize that your child's progress will be wavery. Sometimes you have to beat a strategic retreat—for example, if he gets sick or you have to visit your fastidious Aunt Hannah so you put him back into plastic pants for an afternoon. Sometimes he won't clean up his mess and you end up doing it, though you know you shouldn't because you're being backed into a corner. But company is coming and there's no way out.

Expect that there will be days when he won't clean up, that there will be accidents after he's trained, and that there will be times when you can't see a single reason why he didn't do it in the right place. But don't pull back from your expectation. Despite setbacks, you will find that his own will is your best ally. And the great thing about this method is that it makes toilet training *his* responsibility, not yours. You provide the props, then let him take over.

Gradualness and expectation are the key words. And the process is all.

Children should not be forced to do anything, but "eased" into doing something.

II
Discipline:
Myths and Realities

If you invited a friend over for Sunday brunch and she slopped her tomato juice into her eggs benedict, turned her full cup of coffee over on your good white tablecloth, didn't apologize, rejected every polite suggestion you made, and then made a grab for your new eyeglasses, how would you feel? How devoted to her would you remain?

Chances are your friend never behaved this way. Adults are relatively socialized. That's why they're easier to have as friends. But our children are not our friends—they may be someday, but not now. We didn't select them, and we didn't choose their qualities or even how they looked. We got them, or propagated them, or discovered too late we were having them. Fortunately for the human race, there is something maternal or paternal in most of us, and we are able to be loving at least part of the time.

THE MYTH OF UNLIMITED LOVE

Yet the myth that parents should always feel loving and never feel angry at their children is a fairly pervasive one in our society. It is responsible for a great deal of parental confusion and anxiety. The discrepancy between this perfectionist dream of how parents are supposed to feel and what they truly do feel makes for a lot of misery.

This would not be so hard to take if children would respond to the reasonableness we ask of ourselves with a corresponding reasonableness of their own. But they don't. And the fact that we don't respond when they don't (almost a certainty) derives from the fact that it took us a long time to grow up. There is nothing that can make us regress into infantile behavior more quickly than the infantile behavior of our very own young.

"I'll whomp you but good!" shouts a mother as her son tips over a stand of Campbell soups at the supermarket. With cans rolling in every direction, she is embarrassed, and she wants vengeance and she wants it fast.

Laurie, age two, spread talcum powder all over the living room rug. "Look, Mommy, footprints," she said as she tracked the powder all over the house with her socks and shoes off, toes wiggling in every direction. Next Laurie smeared Vaseline all over the bedroom furniture. "And," she exclaimed with a pleased smile, "I polish." In the face of company coming to dinner in fifteen minutes, her mother could take no more. "I screamed like a banshee while my poor child cowered in a corner," she told me. "What made it worse was the fact that first I was mad at her. Then I was mad at myself. After all, was it her fault? She was only a tiny tot and trying to help." The mother described her unhappy ruminating. "I thought to myself, how could she know it was wrong? And even if she did, maybe she was angry because I'd been gone all morning." By the time Laurie's mother got finished with her inner soliloquy, she had yelled murderously, vacuumed compulsively, apologized profusely, and then found herself in the uncomfortable state of not knowing what the issues were or how to deal with them effectively. An exhausting business.

THE MYTH OF CHILDHOOD INNOCENCE

Laurie's mother was struggling with two not uncommon mixups that frequently cut into reasonable discipline. The first one concerns the child's innocence. Did Laurie or did she not know she was not to do what she had done? At the age of two, perhaps not. But it still was reasonable to remove her, clean the place up, and fume. After all, company was coming and time was short. The mother went further, however, and made the inference that if Laurie didn't know, she was then not responsible for what she had done. From there the mother took the step of blaming herself for being so angry, since she didn't approve of angry mothers. Mothers are supposed to feel loving, right? They are to be helpful and considerate at all times, correct? The issue of Laurie's misbehavior was quite forgotten in all of this. The question of how to educate her to do better was lost in the guilt that confounded the mother because she was so angry.

The second mixup in this mother's reasoning concerned the child's motives. The mother speculated that Laurie might well have been attempting to express a feeling by her behavior. She then made a psychological deduction which took Laurie off the hook a second time. "If she's upset because I left her," thought this modern mother, "then I must be understanding of her motives. Poor darling, it's not her fault."

Either way Laurie's mother approached the problem, her reasoning led to guilty feelings and self-recrimination. She was caught between "She's innocent so it's not her fault" and "She has a reason so I must forgive her." Her scolding of Laurie had a no-yes, no-yes quality. Uncertainty had done her in—and there's nothing like uncertainty to do anyone in. Children are quick to perceive it, and then they move in with steamroller confidence.

What Laurie's mother didn't know was that two-year-olds

are people of little brain.* Whatever the reason for the messing (adorable as it was deemed later in cocktail party conversation), Laurie had made a mess, and her mother needed to
stop her and, in doing so, teach her some restraint. With
more time at her disposal, she could have had Laurie help
her clean up. She could have said, "Sand is for playing;
powder is for baths." The emphasis would then have been on
the act; the responsibility would have been on the child. The
mother's job would be to instruct her, so that she would
know better next time.

The Myth of Childhood Innocence with which this
mother struggled supports the notion that little ones grow
beautifully and naturally if the environment allows them to
develop without interference. As with flowers, tender loving
care is thought to be enough. There is little, if any, recognition of socially unacceptable impulses on the part of the
young. The entire emphasis is on the role the environment
must play to allow growth to emerge unimpeded. But what
this idea does in actual practice is to paralyze parents. They
wait to take their cues from their children, who are really
waiting to take their cues from their parents. Everyone is in
a fog.

THE UNDERSTANDING FALLACY

The second error in reasoning with which this mother
struggled might be labeled the Understanding Fallacy. This
view, unlike the first, acknowledges that children may be
naughty or unreasonable but then *understands why and explains it away.* Once again, response to Junior's behavior gets
lost in excuses ready-made for him.

Three-year-old Lee dumps his chocolate pudding on his
baby sister's head. "It was an accident," coos Grandma sym-
pathetically. "Here." She seizes a cloth. "I'll clean it up."

---

*Unlike Winnie-the-Pooh, however, their gray matter increases with age. A
cheering thought.

Mother, who has read many of the experts' books, bides her time. After all, it's her *husband's* mother, not hers. Later she gently explains to her mother-in-law that Lee is jealous of the new baby. Her mother-in-law, eager to be noninterfering and hence as popular as possible, looks blank. She struggles with a concept hitherto alien to her own child rearing. Are the little dears really capable of the hostility her daughter-in-law is suggesting? It is hard for grandmothers to remember back. If it's true, as Lee's mother says, that behavior has meaning and that a lot of what children do is not haphazard accident—what are parents to do in the face of such behavior? Do children have a right to be aggressive? This is one of the paradoxes in our age of psychological enlightenment. What was meant to be helpful in child rearing (the concept that children are really people, with complex feelings of their own) now is a dilemma for the adults who must rear them.

If mother subscribes either to grandmother's "He doesn't know any better" theory or her own "If he has a reason, he shouldn't be curbed" school of thought, her goose is cooked. If the child becomes aware that the adults in his world don't mean their "don'ts," he can push even harder to find out where the limits really are. Instead of better-behaved children, one gets children who are less well behaved.

The truth is that young children *can* be charming and lovable. I myself find them so, especially when they are asleep. But it is also true that they can be mercilessly demanding and annoying no matter how sweet, understanding, and reasonable you are. A good deal of development has to take place before they learn to be considerate of their fellows. And the adults who raise them must do a good deal of teaching if children are to develop the self-discipline which will enable them to cope when parents are no longer there to oversee.

This is a different view from the one which sees discipline as unnecessary because "man is good" and will be self-disciplined as a matter of course. It is also different from the view which advocates a generally inflexible type of discipline because "man is bad" and needs to have the badness drilled out of him.

CHILDREN ARE NEITHER GOOD NOR BAD

Both of these extremes ignore the basic fact that a young child is incomplete. He has the potential for both goodness and badness but he does not yet have the mental or emotional equipment to make sound choices. He needs older people with more experience to help him along. When he makes mistakes or misbehaves, we have to remember in this age of popular psychology that a reason is not an excuse. A reason may explain why something has happened, but the doer is still responsible for what he does.

Many parents believe that if they set a good example by their own civilized behavior, their children will follow suit. Certainly this is part of the process, but it is by no means all of it. What parents learn, often the hard way, is that good behavior has to be taught.

To begin with, the very young child, adorable as he may be, is a fairly unreasonable creature. While no one ever interviewed a baby, from observation we have divined how self-centered he is. He wants what he wants when he wants it. He appears to be quite certain that the world revolves around his needs. A cry brings a genie bearing food, a whimper brings a change of clothes, a shy smile yields hugs and kisses from giants who kneel before those tiny fingers.

For the preservation of the race, it is good that babies evoke this caretaking from all of us—or they would never survive. Unlike other species, man has a very long childhood and he is dependent for years on his parents or parent substitutes. The interaction of love and affection between the generations (no gap here) helps children to develop the humanity and the caring they will pass on to *their* children, for "love runs downhill."*

But love, as a famous doctor once said, is not enough.** Good conduct has to be taught. In our twentieth-century zeal to individualize children and respond to their needs, we have often overlooked their equally important needs for expectation, limits, and discipline. As a result, many polite, loving, and charming parents are so fearful of being considered "rejecting" (the final, most horrible reproach in our current lexicon of name calling) that they accept anything and everything their children do.

"What can I do with him?" asks a mother helplessly as she sees her five-year-old chase her three-year-old with a hot poker in his hand. "Grab the poker!" I shout, as I seize the three-year-old. "Stop him!"

I see her slowly absorb the idea that small children need limits. (The children are still alive at this writing.) Someone with more sense than a young child has to say "no." The child's very helplessness requires that the adults in charge serve as his steering mechanism for quite a while. The slow and gradual relinquishing of this steering function, as he gets older and is more capable of self-management, is what discipline is all about.

MOTHERHOOD ISN'T SAINTHOOD

The myth that mothers will always be kind, maternal, and patient during this process crumbles before the reality of human fallibility. Motherhood doesn't bequeath sainthood. Those who aspire to the latter may have a rude awakening.

Janie, five, was sent up to bed twenty times in a row. First she was down for a glass of water. Second for her teddy bear. Then the bathroom, Next a kiss to Grandma. Then the bath-

*I am indebted to William Gibson for this phrase, which he uses in his novel *A Mass for the Dead* (New York: Atheneum, 1968).
**Bruno Bettelheim has written a book with this title, *Love Is Not Enough* (Glencoe, Ill.: Free Press, 1950).

room again. A second kiss to Grandma. Her mother remained sweetly reasonable throughout this performance. At the nineteenth request she blew her cool. "How many times have I told you it's time for bed?" Her gentle tones had become a roar. She was shaking now with not-so-suppressed rage.

Five minutes later the final blow came. A curly head peeped over the banister. "If you'd only said 'no' in the first place," said Janie piously, "this wouldn't have happened."

It was this mother's belief in the Myth of Childhood Innocence that put her in this fix. She was patiently waiting for the much-touted goodness to emerge and was setting a good example by her patient and reasonable tone. Janie, on the other hand, wanted what she wanted and even what she didn't want—a characteristic of the five-year-old and under. She needed someone with better sense to set her straight and mean it.

Small children can be untiring in their pushing. As one mother told me, "Give 'em an inch and they'll take a yard. And probably your neighbor's yard as well!" But if you think ahead to where you are going to draw the limits, you can outline your strategy and step in early.

That's where making up your mind that once out of bed for water and the bathroom is enough. Janie was responding to the finality in her mother's voice *then.* It could have happened, as she explained, nineteen times earlier. You do better when you make your expectations clear in the beginning, before you become so angry that nothing short of drawing blood will satisfy you.

RESPONSIBILITY MUST BE TAUGHT

Your child feels safer with structure in his life. I have seen many out-of-control children in my practice, and I find that they are really begging to be stopped. You do better when you stop them sooner rather than later.

The bonuses of this approach are the following:

You are less angry.

He is more lovable.

Parents have argued with me about this point. They've said, "We've tried it. It doesn't work." When I ask them what happened to make their attempts fail, I learn that they tried the rule once, or even twice, but never for the weeks and months that it requires. Their uncertainty about whether they had a right to make their expectations stick showed up in a kind of pleading. Children, as I've said before, catch on pretty quickly. While the parents are waiting for sweet reason to emerge, the children see no cause to give up immediate pleasure unless it is clear to them that they must.

Bruce, four and a half, was told by his mother that he was now old enough to make his bed, take out the rubbish, and clear his dishes at dinnertime. She explained that doing these things would help make him happier when he was an adult.

Several weeks later he referred back to this conversation. "You know those rules you said would make me happier?" he asked. She nodded. "Well," he said emphatically, "they don't."

It takes time to teach responsibility, and your efforts are often not appreciated. Your child needs to know that his parents are in reasonable control of his life for a good many years. Children have few inner controls in the beginning. They learn about them, at first, from you. They are relieved when you take on this responsibility. And, over a period of time, they begin to take your rules and regulations into themselves. A slowly developing conscience (coming from the inside) gets its boost from you (acting on the outside) at a time when conscience is a variable and sometime thing.

The Myth of Natural Goodness (logical sequel to Childhood Innocence) contributes to the confusion of parents, for it robs them of decisiveness in the face of infantile behavior. It also conflicts with our well-documented observations of the egocentric infant. One little boy, age five, told me this quite clearly. He had been brought to see me because of his out-of-control behavior in kindergarten. "I want it all," he said, his arms circling an imaginary globe. "I want to be *first;* I want to be *best;* I want to be the *most loved;* I want to be the *most important.*" His behavior testified to this. He tormented his teacher and his classmates. He couldn't wait, or take a turn, or share a toy.

How do we reason with such a child? How do we help him accept the frustrations that go with recognizing the rights of others? How do we help him face the tensions that come when egocentricity demands modification? In short, how do we help him move from the pleasure principle of babyhood to the reality principle of life?

The next two chapters take up the question of the theory and practice of discipline. They could be titled, "How to Civilize Your Child Without Taking the Joy out of Him or out of You Either."

This book has a particular tone. Tone is the attitude of the author toward the subject and reader. The tone that I feel the author has here is a feeling of responsibility for both parent and child. Wiesburger believes that although the parents are responsible for the upbringing of the child, they must allow the child to become responsible for himself. She explains that this is hard and the parents attempts are not always appreciated and that it is a long process.

III

A Timetable for Discipline

"Everything I do," says Tommy indignantly, "you blame on me." Hands on his hips, eyes close to tears, he is very, very sorry for himself. Yet he cannot join in our laughter. He doesn't see the point.

Two-year-old Mary, having just wet herself, points to her friend Betty accusingly. "Her did it," she says. "Her wet my pants."

The question of who did what is a big one, and the matter of responsibility in some instances may never be resolved satisfactorily. But all parents are confronted by the question of responsibility, and discipline is the means by which they help instill a sense of responsibility in their children.

Discipline, in its most elemental sense, means teaching. The ultimate aim of discipline is to make the child responsible for himself and his behavior. The long-range goal is the child's self-control. The problem then becomes one of how to shift the controls from yourself to him. What makes the situation complicated is that the child is growing and changing all the time. Trying to keep up with him is like trying to catch a moving train. You have to change your expectations as he develops. The signals aren't always clear.

"IT'S JUST A STAGE"

Pediatricians sometimes assuage parents' anxieties about their children's development with the comment, "Don't worry. It's just a stage." They have a point. It is not only the child's bones which are growing but his mind and awareness too. Growth, both physical and emotional, *is* a factor and it is on your side. It proceeds, normally, in the direction of maturity. Many of the quirks of the two-year-old do pass. That the three-year-old only develops new idiosyncrasies can be frustrating. One of the most difficult things for a mother is getting used to this constant change. Just about the time you think you've figured out how to deal with him, he's off on a new kick. It can be pretty exasperating. As the main educator of your child, you are placed in the position of having to teach what you believe is proper behavior. You don't always know how to go about it. Some kids pick up what you expect with little direction. They are the ones who irritate every other mother on the block. Most kids aren't that easy to teach. For your peace of mind, don't compare yourself to the mothers of these paragons. Cultivate the mother who's in worse shape than you are; she could really be a friend.

Helping a child become self-disciplined requires effort. The experts who discuss motherhood as a self-fulfilling experience don't seem to recognize the hard work involved. Teaching is required, and the best kind of teaching occurs when the child sees a connection between what happened and the results which follow. A sequential kind of reasoning, begins to take place.

When a child is very young you have to intervene frequently, and the reasons for your actions may not be clear to him. But you can't let him burn the house down so that he will learn that lighting matches is not a good idea. As he starts to get about on his own, at the end of the first year or the beginning of the second, it's a good idea to toddler-proof the house. This is a sensible recognition of his immaturity. Removing dangerous things ahead of time saves a lot of wear and tear on both of you. As he grows older and gains more impulse control, he will be able to manage better. His safety— which includes putting poisons out of his reach, holding on tightly to his hand as you approach a street crossing, strapping him in when you drive in a car, and the many other things you do to protect him—is not negotiable. His life and his safety require active intervention.

But after you've allowed for the stringent action you take on these issues, you are still confronted by the day-in, day-out disciplining that your child requires. The need for your intervention comes from the normal antisocial feelings that accompany his growth and development.

TEACHING SELF-CONTROL

There are some general concepts of teaching self-control that apply to all ages. Intervention means teaching right from wrong. If your child hits someone or tries to destroy something, he should be stopped. Remove him immediately, if not from the scene, then from the spot. If he goes back for more, take him home. If he's already at home, put him in another room. If he breaks something, explain that he has to make the loss good. Restitution can be made. He can go with you to buy a new vase or he work with you to glue something together. There is a logic in making something good, in fixing up, in undoing a mess. If he embarrasses you while you are out, take him firmly by the hand—or sidesaddle if he puts up a real kick—and leave. No need to put up with supermarket antics. Puffed rice for dinner one night is better than a huge scene at the store. He learns a lot from these sensible consequences that you provide for him. He may not be able to see the larger ones yet, but as you step in as necessity dictates, he does begin to learn. He can be made to sit on a stool until he can manage. He can be sent to his room if he needs time to cool down. He can be told he can join you when he can control himself. The aim is always to put the responsibility on him—where it belongs.

This approach is positive because:

1. It makes the child aware that he is expected to do better.
2. It implies that he has the capacity to improve.
3. It enables him to see the connection between what he did and why he is being stopped.
4. It gives him a chance to think things over without a fight. He can't listen until he's calmed down. Often, when a child is put in his room, he begins to play and defuses by himself.
5. It allows him to rejoin the family when he thinks he can handle things. This gives him some feeling of power over his own destiny. He isn't merely giving in to you; he is meeting a social demand when he is able. The urge for self-control is given a boost since he likes himself better when he manages well.

This approach is also positive because it does *not:*

1. Hurt his feelings—at least not for very long.
2. Encourage the nursing of grievances and the desire for revenge.
3. Clear the air so swiftly he can promptly forget about it. (In one instance, Stephen, eight, was sent to me because he seemed to ask for spankings. He agreed that this was so. "It's simple," he said. "When I get one, it wipes the slate clean. It's my ticket to start over." He felt that he had paid—not learned, but paid.)
4. Set up a contest in which he ends up feeling like a loser.

The real battle for self-control is within the child himself. Partly he wants to grow up and do more; partly he likes what is easy, infantile, and familiar. If you allow this issue to get lost in a fight between the two of you, you end up taking the responsibility for what is his responsibility after all. Remember that the important argument is not between you and your child. It is between the child's two conflicting feelings. The ping-pong match should be with himself.

PUNISHMENT

A time-honored method of discipline is punishment. That is, you instill fear into a child in the belief that this will deter him from future nefarious activity. It may. Parents have told me that spankings clear the air. I believe they often do. But I don't think it is the inflicting of pain which does the trick. Rather, what happens is that the child finally perceives that the parents truly mean what they say. Most often, spankings come as a last resort. We are at our wits' end. Nothing has worked, and we are really beyond reason ourselves. By this time we may want to inflict a little pain, especially because we are feeling so much of it ourselves.

Here teaching has been lost as everyone is out of control. A fight has ensued, with you the winner because you are bigger. One father told me with pride that he had thrashed his eight-year-old, who had hit a three-year-old, within an inch of his life. "I'll teach him," he said, "to pick on someone smaller." Right.

If you plan ahead for the worst contingencies, you are taken less by surprise and are therefore less likely to spank. You are also less likely to threaten punishment that you won't deliver. If you do have to come down hard in the face of provocation, your response won't be out of proportion to the situation.

MAKING A PLAN

Making a plan may mean sitting down with your husband in a quiet spot and thinking over what is appropriate for your child at his age. Going out to eat and talk things over often helps both of you to be more objective. When you are both clear about what you expect of your child, you can then make it clear to him. If you tell him ahead of time and give him sufficient warning ("We have to leave in half an hour so start getting ready"), he has time to switch gears and prepare himself.

The rules of the game are expectation, consistency, and stopping him when he can't manage. If you keep changing the rules on him, he'll be confused. You may be skeptical about whether this system works because you've seen your child repeatedly delay the family by refusing to be ready on time. Or you've seen him make a mess at someone's home and refuse to clean it up.

But you do have a surprising ally in all of this—your child himself. He has a wish to be good, to grow up and master things. Stopping him from behavior which is not socially acceptable enables his better self to win. It encourages the child's self-esteem, because there is pride in virtue. A child likes himself better when he knows he's done the right thing. On the other hand, all human beings, big or little, get angry sometimes. Once we accept this fact we can begin to deal with the less than beautiful feelings more realistically.

Every parent has his own style. Some parents grew up with spankings and are not comfortable with other methods. Others try the "Get in early before you are unhinged" approach and find that it works. All parents, however, will help their children grow in the right direction by setting a goal ahead of time—say, for the next three months—and then requiring that it be met. The first step is to select the issues that are important to you. These vary from family to family. But you have the right to insist on what matters most to you. Once you have done so, you will find yourself able to be flexible about matters which don't mean so much to you. This flexibility helps the long-term firmness which is required.

Special problem areas run the gamut of childish orneriness. Holding the line on the issue that bothers your family the most is the best place to begin. It could be the bedtime issue that you choose to take up; it could be mealtime shenanigans; it could be changing clothes after school or, with older children, doing homework before watching television in the evening. It could be any problem which upsets your particular family.

When you choose the one which bugs you *the most,* stay with your expectations on that point over a period of time. And remember that you can't deal effectively with more than one big problem at a time. If you go at a number of them, the child feels he's being nagged and soon learns to tune you out. Staying consistently with the one problem, for months if necessary, will simplify life for the whole family in the long run. More important, the success achieved in one area will begin to spread to other issues. The carryover occurs because the child has mastered something in himself in the process of dealing successfully with one issue. It's as though he's developing moral muscle when he succeeds in behaving better. Try to remember that the young child will do what is right as long as someone he cares about insists on it. Later, when he begins to adopt many of your values as his own, you will be able to lessen your active involvement.

Backsliding will occur occasionally, since home is not the army. But if the trend is in the right direction, you'll make your point. A good general rule, when you're choosing the issues which are helpful for his development, is never to do for a child what he's able to do for himself. A lot of nonsense gets eliminated by observing this rule. A lot of infantile tyranny dissipates.

SAYING VS. DOING

Good children come from all sorts of homes—strict, casual, and in between. Whatever the home environment, it does not hurt them to be asked to fit in. You can hear little ones out; you can listen to complaints; you can even ask them for their ideas about what they can do to fulfill your demands. *But it is your judgment which prevails when you think something is right.* They do not yet have the overall picture, and it is important for you not to yield on something which you feel is not desirable for them.

"My Mommy means it," said four-year-old Lucy proudly to a friend. What she meant was that she appreciates her mother's caring enough about her to risk facing Lucy's displeasure. Wanting to be loved by a child can make you afraid to be firm. Don't let it! Remember how your favorite teachers were strict but fair? Children feel safer with clear-cut limits. While our ideal is to be rational and to give our children sensible reasons for what we expect of them, this can often be overdone. A clear "Because I said so" is often as reasonable as you can get, given the demands of family life.

This latter point raises an issue that bedevils all parents. One mother said to me, "If I let her say it, does it mean I let her do it?" The answer is no, you don't. The little girl can voice her jealousy of her baby brother. "I wish you'd take him back where you got him," she says angrily. She can announce that he is a pest and that she'd like to push him out a window. "But I won't let you," you tell her. "You can feel it and say it, but you can't do it."

This is the ultimate restraint. The talking provides a channel for the unacceptable feeling, but the controls are still coming from you. Some parents are reluctant to encourage children to voice their feelings in the fear that it will open a Pandora's box of bad behavior. On the contrary. The hurt and/or angry feelings are there anyhow. The acceptable outlet of talk can prevent mayhem, as it offers a release of pressure. By saying "We don't hit" and "I won't let you hurt me" and "Go to your room until you can manage," you put the lid on the behavior. At the same time, by showing the child that you understand, you make his difficult feelings easier to bear. Stories which illuminate a point for children are a great help in this connection (see Chapter VII).

The general timetable given below, which you should regard with the same flexibility as those on physical development that are to be found in every baby book, can help you to tailor your expectations to the age of the child. What is appropriate behavior for a two-year-old is not necessarily appropriate for a three-year-old. You expect more as your child grows older. The next chapter will examine the specific behavioral difficulties that most parents encounter.

THE FIRST YEAR OF LIFE

Nature has a neat system. Baby cries and you respond. Baby is appeased; you are delighted. Slowly you begin to catch on to what he is asking for. You feel more competent and able to decipher his signals. You become the great tension reliever, feeder, diaper changer, hurt soother, cuddler, burper, path clearer, and many other things you'd never anticipated. What you are doing the first year, in general, is responding to him. The weaning which takes place in the second half of the first year is gradual. This is the first "takeaway" he encounters, and you don't want to hurry it. One feeding at a time gets dropped; there is a gradual transition to cup. Babies tend to be conservative in that they like only what they know, so that gradualness in all things—whether in weaning, toilet training, introducing new babysitters, or visiting the doctor—is important. Babies are less upset when the changes go slowly.

In general, you are enjoying your child's babyhood and responding to his needs as he is feeling them. The mother-child unit begins to happen. Just as your responsiveness supports his developing maturity, so his responsiveness is turning you into a mother. The taking care promotes the caring.

On the other hand, you are never free for a moment. How

could one baby take so much time? After you have two or more children, you wonder what kept you so busy with the first. This relates to a famous dictum (apologies to Parkinson's Law): Baby or babies take all available time.

Slowly, in the first year they learn to know you. And, when they do, they want only you. So you are really hooked. Now when baby cries, you hurt. He has become more important than you ever anticipated. Yet he can make you so mad you sometimes want to wring his little neck. He wails; he teethes; he's prone to stuffy noses and other uncomfortable ailments. To make it harder, most of the time you have to guess about what will please him because he can't tell you. All mothers are certain, at some point or another, that there is something they could be doing to stop tears or ease a problem, if they only knew what it was. Mostly, all you can do, at these anxious times, is to live through them. Don't be surprised if you feel upset; there's nothing more irritating than not being able to relieve a child's misery. Talking to other mothers and sharing frustrations can help you to tolerate the bad days when you feel cut off from the outside world and your baby isn't responding to your ministrations. The knowledge that "this too shall pass," that your child *will* grow beyond this, will help to sustain you.

At around seven or eight months he may scream at the sight of a new face. Try to remember that this is a compliment, for he can now tell that the other people he sees are not his mother. Still, the experience can be unnerving. Leaving him with a sitter at this time may be harder than it was when he was first born. This doesn't mean that you are never to leave him with a sitter. (See Chapter VIII for a full discussion on separation.) But there are some helpful things you can do. Try to have a sitter with whom the baby becomes acquainted over a period of time. He relates, then, to a familiar person. If you need to hire a new sitter, have her come over a day or two before you leave, or at least an hour or so early, while you are still there, so he can get used to her in your safe presence. At this age, the child should not be left for too long an interval. An afternoon away is as much as he can stand during the first year. He has no sense of time and often his frantic cries reflect his feeling that he'll never see you again. When you leave, always say good-by, even though you are aware that his comprehension is fairly dim. He begins to grasp, through experience, that you do not disappear permanently. Short absences of a few hours teach him the realities and give him a chance to cope because they're not overwhelming in length.

In the second half of the first year small changes begin to appear. Your child becomes restless when he is held; he squirms when you diaper him. He is more interested in things; he examines objects with an intensity he didn't show before. He wants to do more for himself—grasping, sitting, pulling himself up, creeping, standing. He loves mastering new things, and feeding himself is a step in this direction. You may need some reassurance to see self-feeding as progress, what with oatmeal mush all over his highchair and runny gelatin on his hands and face. I recommend newspapers on the floor, a big bib under his chin, and a towel to mop him up with, so that he can enjoy these pleasures of touch and taste without too much interference. Even at this early age you can encourage his independence by not doing for him what he can do for himself. From being the all-important provider of the first six months, you have to become the allower and encourager of the second six months. Babies have an inner drive toward independence and mastery and they need to express it, even though they may become more difficult to handle.

ONE TO TWO YEARS OF AGE

In this year big changes take place. He is not only walking, but talking; furthermore, he is understanding much more than he can say. Maturation has gone on swiftly, and he's really no longer a baby. He looks like a baby to you because you're so close to him, but it's important that you recognize he is ready for much more from you than the responsive care of the first year. He now has so much motor power that you wonder why you ever wished him out of the playpen. What he hasn't got is much in the way of steering ability. You will be doing most of the piloting with your "yesses" and "nos." Your decor may start to look like early warehouse, as your knick-knacks and art objects disappear into a back closet. However, retreating temporarily in this fashion makes sense, because he doesn't have much ability to control his impulses. You are saying "no" a lot at this age, because he's into everything. What aggravates you is the deliberate provocation in some of his behavior. He can eye you mischievously as he carefully and obviously does the forbidden. Mostly this means he is testing for limits, and stopping him helps him to learn.

Distracting him with other things also helps a great deal. Eventually he gets too smart for this kind of maneuver, so that you have to move on to other methods. If you use distraction beyond this early time—say, after the age of three —it can easily turn into manipulation. You have a right to stand your ground when you know he comprehends.

On the other hand, knowing what to overlook is equally valuable. There are advantages to letting some things pass when they are not important. It lets you keep your ammunition for what really counts. It's important to have things around that he is allowed to handle, as this reduces the number of no-nos and makes for greater overall tranquility. Here alternatives make sense. Pots, pans, and sturdy toys are useful, since at this time of life the child is busy testing, biting, and banging. Clay and water play are helpful because toddlers enjoy making messes. Don't worry about cleanups at this time; he's still too young for these. The toilet training in the second half of the first year is the major accomplishment of this period; it is the first time a consistent and absolutely necessary expectation has been made of him. His meeting that expectation with pride gives a spurt to later independence. The cleanups that toilet training require are enough for him to handle for the time being.

One of the benefits of the toilet-training method recommended in the first chapter is that other cleanups (toys, clothes, and so on) *eventually* are less of a fight because he has made progress in conquering his own messy self. Learning to master body messes leads to more generalized orderliness. One mother, after toilet training was completed, was flabbergasted to see her three-year-old daughter put her toys away spontaneously. The yes-no struggle about responsibility had been won early in another, more basic arena.

The increasing ability to talk is a great assist. A child is less frustrated when he can make his wishes clear, and action gets modified when wishes get voiced. One fragile thing now may come out of the back closet. You say "no" to him so that he slowly learns to control himself. He seems able to grasp what you mean, although often he appears to have little intention of abiding by the rules. The importance of your clearness about what's "yes" and what's "no," however, cannot be overstressed. The steering is still largely yours, but he is taking it all in. These are building blocks for self-control. Gradually, to your delighted surprise, he may even begin to say "no" to himself. If you find he can't manage to resist this treasure, take it away and try again in a few months. This process recognizes the contribution of maturation to discipline.

TWO TO THREE YEARS OF AGE

Somebody has described the "terrible twos" as running from eighteen months to three years. The negativism that occurs in this period cuts across neat age classifications. As with all categories which describe human behavior, there's a lot of give at either end. You will recognize the terrible twos *whenever* they appear, for he says "no" to everything. You have to remind yourself repeatedly that what seems like negativism is really the toddler's pride in his developing sense of self.

"Don't you want to see Grandma?"

"No!"

"Don't you want to put on your nice new coat?"

"No!"

If you firmly take him by the hand, he will put on his hat and coat without a struggle and go along with you. Here actions speak louder than words.

What he means by his "no" is that he is his own person. After all, he has his own locomotion now and can get away from you. He can thwart this big giant who seems to be the boss of everything. The important message to you is not to take him too seriously at this age. You don't want to get into a round of fighting over things that don't matter. He wants to make things a contest, but you don't have to. The less you get involved with his "I won'ts" the better for everybody. Here is a time when letting some things slide actually works. When it comes to things that really count, you are bigger and you are the boss and it's okay to make your point.

Until the age of three most toddlers are not truly ready for interactional play with others. It is not that they don't enjoy being with other children. They do, at least for short periods of time. But most children under three indulge in parallel play. They look like they're playing with others but they're really playing side by side. The possessive antisocial behavior the toddler shows about his possessions (toys, mother, *anything*) is par for the course until three or more. Don't wear yourself out trying to teach your child sharing before he is old enough to be able to cope with the garden-variety "I'm for me first" feelings. Of course, it doesn't hurt him if you work toward sharing and taking turns, but recognize that your successes will be tiny until he's closer to three.

On the other hand, hitting, biting, kicking, and grabbing

are out. Don't hesitate to pick him up and put him some-where else. Once again, stopping and removal work best. Talking about it after he calms down helps link the idea with the action. He is more able to tolerate a direct confrontation as he approaches three. He also shows some signs of having heard your prohibitions.

Andy, three, was heard to say to himself as his hand stretched toward a forbidden candy bar, "No, no! Andy mustn't." His mother's prohibition could be heard in his voice. Whether he could summon the strength to *really* resist was less the issue than that he had heard her and was trying to meet her standards. Most children of this age waver a great deal. Sometimes immediate pleasure wins; sometimes they can hold off. One way to help manage this with the two-to-three-year-old toddler is to voice the conflict for him. "Sometimes Andy wants to do what Mommy says; some-times Andy wants to do what *he* wants."

Occasionally his provocation is hard to handle. His eyes dance delightedly as he tests you. He is trying to make a contest out of your prohibition. You might try saying firmly, "I don't want you to do that." Then leave the room. This allows the struggle to be his. Often he complies because you have taken the challenge out of it. You can always remove him if this doesn't work.

Refusing to be provoked by orneriness is easier said than done. Sometimes when you see yourself caught in a daily tangle with an autocratic toddler, you can consider whether it might not be better to sidestep some unprofitable struggles. Helping him save face may ease the hardline stance you both find yourselves in.

"You can be the boss of wearing your hat," you say, or "of eating your carrot" or "of carrying your bear or elephant." He is old enough now to enjoy a decision that's his alone. "But we do have to go," you add, "so you decide about it now."

"I don't want my hat," says Jennifer as she takes it off and marches defiantly out the door. Some of the win-lose sting has been defused.

Be aware that a two-year-old's ability to stay with things is limited. Keep your visiting activities brief, unless your hosts are equipped and willing. Fatigue works against good behavior, so try to give your child his rest. Naps help him to tolerate the daily fray. When he starts to resist napping, set up a daily silent time. He can be permitted books and quiet toys in bed. If he flatly refuses bed, you might permit him to play quietly on the couch or floor. It is important that you separate from each other. If he complains about rest time, set a timer and insist on relative quiet until the bell rings. You might have toys available which are only used during these periods. He won't be happy if you are enjoying yourself too much, however, so keep your own enjoyment of these times a secret.

THREE TO FOUR YEARS OF AGE

Three to four is a great age for nursery school, if you can arrange it. A neutral teacher, with less of an emotional investment in the child, helps in the teaching of appropriate behavior. Cooperative nurseries, where mothers take turns, serve the same function. If neither of these is open to you, try to arrange for your child to play regularly with a small group of children. Learning to play with others is an ongoing process, and he is more ready for the give and take of social life than he was before. At this age too he can pick up his toys and do other simple chores such as emptying a waste basket and putting out napkins. A place to play with a chance to let off steam is good for both of you. Physical activity in a playground or yard is pleasurable for him and helps the discipline process.

Up until this point, you have talked with him primarily about real things in his life. He relates to objects and to people in a fairly concrete way. You may have talked about feelings to him, but you have been uncertain about how much has penetrated. Now he can begin to tell you his feelings as you encourage verbalization. You say, until you are sick of the sound of your own voice, "Tell me, tell me in words." If he is angry, reply to his complaints realistically. If his demand is unrealistic, don't alter your position. It's important not to retreat in the face of childish blandishments, infantile tempers, or manipulative hanky-panky. You may be able to help him accept your firm stand by telling him, "I know it's hard for you." Your understanding can ease the angry, hurt, or frightened feelings.

You are not encouraging feelings as good in and of themselves. They exist in your child as in all human beings; the idea is to make them manageable. As they are verbalized, he can get a handle on them. Hearing himself speak allows him to cope better and manage more successfully. It aids the civilizing process.

When Jimmy was two, he would shout, as he thrashed about, "I'm bangy."

At three, Jimmy would glare at his mother menacingly, as he grew angrier and angrier, and yell, "I'm getting bangy." He was recognizing a familiar feeling and giving fair warning. His growing knowledge of his feelings allowed him to put on his coat as she'd requested. Before he had the words to make his point, he often banged his fists and head against the wall. The improvement in his ability to recognize where his feelings were headed was noticeable in this six-month period of development.

The issues of expectation and the setting of limits as they have been described here may seem reasonable to you. The rub comes in the contradictory nature of your child's progress.

"He seems to go two steps forward, one step back," said one mother to me recently. Every advance seems fraught with a yes-no quality. Just as he learns something new, he seems to forget old skills. Do you remember the irritability that showed itself before he walked or talked? Going from two naps to one made him cranky, as he missed the second nap. Yet if he napped twice he was up all night. Going from one nap to none brought the same cross behavior. Once he mastered the new he was okay until the next step.

The child himself seems not to know which way to go. Often he can't agree with himself. Children frequently show a wish to be babied and a conflicting desire to be grown up. "When I grow up," says Sara, "I want to be a baby." But don't deny the child the right to be responsible. Let it happen.

"My son tells me he can't change his clothes. He acts helpless, wanting me to do it for him. When I don't, he cries and acts forlorn." This mother had thought that being firm would make her little boy feel unloved, since her expectations seemed to make him so miserable. When she learned not to play the game, she was amazed at how pleased he was with his own success. "Why then did he fight me so during the process?" she asked. Part of the answer lies in the fact that children prefer what they've known. The new step is threatening until it is mastered.

Again, it helps to voice a conflict for a child when he is going through a struggle. Tell him, "Part of you wants to be a baby; part of you wants to be grown up." Instead of fighting with you, he learns the battle is within him. The yes-no struggle reflects the inner battle that young children have in growing up. While you support the more mature requirements of good behavior, you help him verbalize his baby longings. A good principle to remember is that he does better when you align yourself with the part of him that wants to grow up. Throwing your weight in this direction is always to the good. Insisting that he do what you know he can do is realistic, and he respects you and himself more as you maintain your expectations. Your voicing the less mature wishes gives acknowledgment to his infantile side, thereby diminishing its intensity.

FOUR TO FIVE YEARS OF AGE

Between four and five the child's world expands immeasurably. Friendships develop; play is more genuinely interactional and more reasonable. You try to help him meet the new and varied expectations that are being made of him. You end by being his backup as he tackles the new and, therefore, the hard. You teach him to cross a street. You show him how to tie his shoes. He can take a bath by himself (bubble bath soaks off what he misses). When he wants to try something more adult, you let him do it, if it's within reason and if you see the justification for it. In these and many other ways you are supporting the development of a self that slowly but surely is becoming independent of you. Safety is, of course, a major factor, and you have a right to be protective.

"You cannot swing from the high swing."

"No, you may not walk on the railroad ties."

He still counts on your judgment, so feel free to wield it, even though he may balk and answer back.

Encouraging this new independence can sometimes be difficult. Four-year-old Nancy was upset about going to nursery school after an easy initiation. Her mother was bewildered. "Do I make her go?" she asked me.

"Is it a good school?"

"Excellent."

"Do you like the staff?"

"Very much," she said.

"Do you think going to this school is a good experience for Nancy?"

"No doubt about it."

I suggested that she tell Nancy she would like to hear more about why she didn't want to go. Perhaps she could confer with the teacher. But at the same time Nancy was to be told, "You have to go to nursery school. Daddy and I think it's good for you." This was not rampant authoritarianism; it was a wiser judgment than Nancy was able at her age to muster. Allowing her to express her feelings helped Nancy to cope without encouraging regression.

Holding the line is not easy for parents. In the middle of such everyday happenings as broken washing machines, delayed plumbers, mother-in-law visits, and laid-off husbands, clear reasoning about normal child development may be hard to come by. Having more than one child brings several sets of tracks—all, it seems, going off in different directions. There are times when you will be boxed into doing some things for your child that he can do for himself, in the interest of expediency and mental health (yours). There are times when yielding is an absolute necessity. Forgive yourself at such moments and get him back into training when things settle down. At frazzling times an afternoon away in adult company can do a lot to restore your equilibrium. Visiting friends who have young children is also helpful, not only for the company but for the commiseration: you realize, with some satisfaction, that the same hassles are going on elsewhere.

IV
Discipline:
Specific Behavior
Problems

Despite the best of intentions, there are some things you cannot make your child do.

You cannot make your child eat.

You cannot make him sleep.

You cannot make him perform body functions.

When he is of school age you cannot make him study.

In every one of these cases it's the old story: "You can lead a horse to water, but you can't make him drink."

Parents, in a genuine concern over nutrition, have sometimes forced their children to eat; and their children have promptly vomited the food right back up. Wooing sleep, as most adults know all too well, is something that must be done by the sleeper himself. While toilet training is a normal process which I heartily espouse, in the last analysis the child himself must actually perform in the right place. The same is true of learning in school in the later years. You can buy a lovely home, provide a great room for your child to work in, select a handsome desk and the best sightsaving lamp, and he can sit amid this splendor and read a comic book or daydream.

Knowing your limitations in regard to these issues can spare you a lot of grief. It is a waste of effort and a sore test of your patience to take responsibility for those matters in which your child is the final arbiter. What can be done, as in toilet training, is setting the scene so that he, who has the final say anyhow, will handle the issue in a way which is constructive for him.

EATING

Physicians who have studied nutrition have learned that children will eat what their bodies require, providing (and this is a big if) that they do not fill themselves up with junk between meals. You can eliminate a lot of the nagging that goes on at many tables in America by serving food and then pretty much ignoring what the kids do with it. No, you don't have to put up with their slinging the peas or daubing their siblings with mashed potatoes. Removal is the best technique for dealing with that kind of nonsense. What I am talking about here is your concern over what they ingest. It's not that important. Milk drinkers, imbibing as they are the near-perfect food, often eat next to nothing. Food eaters often boycott milk. In addition, there are plateau periods of growth where children simply do not eat very much at all. Then at other times they gorge. Nature really takes care of the growth process, and it's a mistake to get too involved in it. If you begin to care too much, as with the toilet-training process, the child will learn how much he can control you with his response to your offerings. Let your doctor tell you if he's deficient in anything.

Limit snacks to regular times of day—say, midmorning or afternoon—and keep a moderate supply of crackers or cookies around to serve with milk or juice. Don't keep fillers like potato chips, pretzels, and candy around. They simply tempt palates which are then too sated to appreciate your hamburgers. Eliminate the bickering by eliminating the temptation. If your husband wants some snacks to go with his beer at night, tuck some away for him.

When you serve a meal, give your child advance notice. "In fifteen minutes I'll call you in for lunch." When he comes in, serve it. If he complains that he doesn't like this or that, say, "Okay, then don't eat it." If he wants only dessert, let him have it. If you're very concerned about his nutrition, stick to fruits, puddings, ice cream, or gelatin for dessert. This doesn't mean he is winning a battle and that you are contributing to the weakening of his manly fiber. It does mean that you are not making a moral issue out of a natural process. Why should ice cream be less valued than broccoli? It too is highly nutritious. It is we who make these value judgments by announcing, "You don't get your dessert unless you eat your vegetables." When the fight goes out of it, children generally eat all foods better.

Do *not* become a short-order cook. If he doesn't want to eat at mealtime, place his plate in the refrigerator. If he's hungry later, he can have it then. If he complains that the meal is cold, do not heat it up. If he wants a hot meal, he will have to learn to eat it when it's served. Here too the consequences are built in. If he misses a meal, ignore it. He'll just eat more heartily the next time.

As he gets older and displays a few marked food aversions, such as hating liver or getting a rash from fish, you can allow him to make a sandwich for himself when you serve these foods. The point is not to disturb the rest of the family but to recognize an individual bias when it is legitimate. Removing food as an arena for argument makes children less scrappy in general, so that on the issues where you really have to hold the line, they are more amenable to reason— as you are.

If you feel that you cannot offer dessert without your child's earning it (the Puritan ethic seems caught up in this for a lot of people), what you can do is serve family style. Family-style meals help to create a pleasant atmosphere, since children select what and how much of something they want. Allow the child to take his own helping from the family serving dish—as little or as much as he wishes. It is then his obligation to finish what he has chosen if he is to receive dessert. This is a second-best plan (the best is not caring at all), but it may be as much as you can undertake, considering the way your parents dealt with you.

SLEEPING

Bedtime requires a similar approach. Deciding ahead of time on an hour which is suitable for your family is a good beginning. Sticking to it may be hard, as children "spoil" easily in this area. Staying up with him at night during an illness may have him insisting afterward that you prolong your stay in his room. Get him back at once on an "out for a drink and bathroom" regimen, and that is it. Be oblivious to crocodile tears. If he complains he can't sleep, put a lamp near his bed and let him have some quiet playthings, such as cuddle toys, books, crayons, and paper. This lets him wind down, and you may often find him fast asleep over his toys in a few minutes. Naptime can produce similar resistance as a child gets older. Insist on a quiet time, allow for some play in bed, and place a timer in his room to let him know when he can leave.

Serenity has been defined as having an alternative. If he can't sleep, give him an alternative by permitting quiet play. Here again you set the rules and arrange the props; he performs the act. Once he starts school, he may try to beat the system by staying up to read. But here you win for losing because he is becoming a reader. In general, quiet times before bed are best; roughhousing should be kept to a minimum. There is nothing wrong with a toss in the air if the child enjoys it. Fathers often think this is a good way to relate to children and carry it further with tussling and wrestling. They think roughhousing makes men out of boys. But often children find it too stimulating, and sleep disturbances result. If you see this happening, try more quiet play before bedtime.

Fathers can make contact with their children without over-stimulating them. They can read them stories and help them with puzzles, and play other games with them when they are older.

Sports during the day are another matter, but children are better off engaging in sports activities with those of their own age. This puts them in a less disadvantaged position. For the child under five, games of chance generally are better than games requiring skill. In skill games competition with an adult is unfair, and it doesn't make sense for an adult to pretend to lose. In games of chance (like the various spin-the-wheel games) everyone is equal before the odds. The child may lose, but he may just as easily win. Hold off on skill games until the child is of school age, when he is more capable of grasping the concepts involved.

The issue of watching TV before bedtime is not a simple one. Each family has its own constellation of interests and must decide about TV for itself. Yet there is no question that television sets up an artificial situation in which children are bombarded with stimulating material but are placed in the position of receiving it passively. For this reason children often indulge in thumbsucking, masturbating, eating, and nervous mannerisms while watching TV. The tensions, which have been artificially engendered by the media, have no place else to go. Cutting down on afterdinner viewing usually makes sleep easier. When you have a big family, this may be difficult to do. You are faced with individual preferences and who watches what, when. One mother of five got so fed up with TV bickering that she outlawed TV on school nights. She okayed it on Fridays and Saturdays, and the group voted on which shows were to be seen. She could not believe how much wrangling she eliminated in this way. What surprised her most was how relieved the children seemed to be and how easily they accepted her decision. Apparently a lot of covert sibling rivalry (endless in any family anyhow) found its way to the surface in the fight over choosing programs. With children under five it is easier to be selective because the good children's programs are fairly obvious.

STUDYING

The same principles which are applicable to body self-control apply to the issue of learning when the child enters school. Once again, your primary task is to provide an environment that will allow the child to take over the function for himself. Just as only the eater can eat, sleeper can sleep, and toilet trainee can train himself, so only the student can learn.

A boy in third grade came home one day with a note from his teacher. She was irate about his poor performance on an arithmetic test. When his mother criticized him, he argued his case plaintively, "But you never took the arithmetic problems out of my pocket!" He needed to be told that school was his business and that homework was his responsibility. In our zeal to help children learn, we have often confused the issue of responsibility. Our wish to rescue children from failure stems from the best of kindly impulses. Certainly there is nothing wrong with being available to help a child if he asks for it. But learning is clearly something he has to do for himself, and it doesn't help him when we accept it as our job. When he isn't doing well, confrontation by the teacher can be constructive for him. After all, it is she who is in a position to assess his problems realistically. As parents we can be sympathetic to his feeling of failure, but we help him best when we ask him what *he* is going to do about it. Even well-meant tutoring will not help if the child has no intention of cooperating.

Throughout a child's life the issues of reality and responsibility have to be balanced against immediate pleasure and gratification. Here again, consequences teach best. An early failure in school, if it's warranted, and repeating a grade can often have sanguine results. Admittedly, you will find it difficult to let this happen to your child because you care about him so much and hate to see him hurt. It will help you when hard decisions have to be made to know that self-esteem comes from within. When a child masters something hard for himself, his pleasure in himself is genuine.

Performing in school is an area in which every parent has an investment. As with other types of behavior, it still remains intrinsically up to your child. You cannot make these behaviors happen. You can help your child let them happen.

However, there is a form of behavior over which you have to exert control—namely, antisocial behavior. You have control over whether your child is *permitted* to carry out his antisocial impulses. You are not only bigger. You have more awareness of what is right and what is wrong. Ultimately, you hope your child will take your views to heart and make them his own. But during the early years it is you who must step in and actively teach. Aggression in children takes many forms, not all of which have been recognized by parents. Fighting, of course, is the most clearly recognizable and may require your intervention if other children are being abused.

FIGHTING

The hitter or biter or scratcher is demonstrating behavior which is *actively* antisocial. Stopping the child and/or removing him from the spot works best. Getting him to talk about his anger when he cools down is helpful, for moving from action to words is a more mature development.

"Danny is mad," you say, as you label his feelings for him. "No, you cannot hit a person," you add. "People hurt when you hit them. Tell me when you're angry." If the child is very young, you can provide an inanimate substitute for him to hit, making the point that things, unlike people, don't *feel.*

If you find him tormenting an animal, stop that too.

"I think I'm raising a sadist," complained one father to me

about his three-year-old daughter. She had been dragging the cat around, kicking it, and pulling its tail unmercifully. She was having a difficult time restraining herself in the tumult of a large family.

After some consideration, her father arranged to have the cat stay with a friend. "When you can manage not to hurt it, you can have your pet back," he told her. After several trial visits at home, the cat was allowed reentry. Margie managed better with each successive visit and her pleasure in her growing self-control was evident.

When your child is older, the sequence will progress from actions to words to thoughts. He will then have the capacity for trial action by means of thought. He can *think* he'd like to slug his friend who received a bigger present, but he won't *do* it. Thinking can both *allow* the antisocial idea and *prohibit* the acting out of the idea. The child will then be able to behave in a more mature way under stress. In kindergarten children are described as immature when they erupt into action every time they are frustrated. The delay that talk or thought brings is not available to them, and their learning is impaired as long as action takes over immediately. If the child has had practice in expressing himself, he has greater ability to delay inappropriate responses. Helping your child to tolerate some frustration aids his developing maturity. You can voice his upset.

"You wish you knew how to ride a bike. When you are older you will be able to."

"No, you must wait your turn."

"It's hard not to get what you want this minute."

The kindergarten teacher will be grateful if your child has learned to tie his shoes before he starts school, but she will be even more grateful if he has learned to tolerate some delay, listen to some instructions, and postpone a demand if necessary.

Hitting back if one is attacked is another question. Most parents see this as reasonable response for self-respect and self-protection. What gets sticky is when the child says he was attacked first but he wasn't; then you are pressed to make a judgment about something you know little about. When you can't find the real culprit in a free-for-all, send everyone to different parts of the house to calm down. There are many battles which end up ambiguously, and a "so what" attitude on your part will probably save your sanity. "I don't care who did what," you find yourself saying. "Just cut it out!"

If you should happen to punish indiscriminately without knowing the facts, the child who is innocent will feel he has been treated unjustly, and your reputation for fairness will suffer. Stopping the children, scattering them, and allowing their anger to subside clears the air better. These storms are generally of short duration, and often the children are pals again before you've had time to regain your equilibrium.

DAWDLING

The dawdler is of another breed entirely. He doesn't appear to be aggressive at all. He just takes twenty minutes to get a sock on, keeps you waiting while he searches vaguely for his gloves, or pulls a sweater on in cinematic slow motion while you steam. "He's a dreamer," you tell your friends. The inference is that he's thinking long, important thoughts. But he can certainly move fast enough when he wants to. What is going on here? He makes you furious, but you can't put your finger on it. After all, he hasn't actually *done* anything—or has he?

My answer is that he has. He hasn't actively driven you out of your mind; he has done it passively. So innocently, so slowly, so seemingly not doing much of anything; and yet you are wild. My advice is to trust your gut reaction. Looking at his behavior objectively, you will see that he had plenty of time in which to be ready. He isn't ready. He provoked your anger by his delaying tactics; he has goaded you. That is really as open a challenge as outright defiance.

Eight-year-old Linda and her family lived right around the corner from her school, yet her mother had to wake her at six every morning to be ready for class at eight-forty. It took her half an hour to brush her teeth. Putting on underwear was a laborious task. At every step her mother reminded, prodded, and exhorted. The battle had to be rewon daily.

Things changed when Linda was told it was her business to get to school. Going to school was the law. She was given an alarm clock, which was realistically set for seven-forty-five; her mother retreated to a back bedroom. The first day Linda, at eight-twenty-five, was sitting in her pajamas waving to her friends who were on their way to school. Mother almost had apoplexy but instead had a third cup of coffee.

As her mother and I talked, she realized how her daughter had blackmailed her.

"But what if she doesn't have time to eat?" she asked, alarmed.

"Is she thin?"

"Oh, no. If anything, she's on the chubby side."

"Good. She can lose weight at the same time."

"But suppose she's late for school?"

"What then?"

"Why, she'll get a tardy slip!" Mother looked horrified.

Linda never did get a tardy slip. One day the policeman at the corner stopped her mother. "Say, listen," he said. "Is Linda your kid?"

She acknowledged that she was.

He scratched his head in a puzzled way. "What is it with her anyway?" he asked. "Every morning she walks like molasses to the corner. And then," he added with a bewildered look, "she turns the corner and beats it like a bat out of hell right to school!"

There are times, of course, when ignoring the dawdler will be impossible. You must be somewhere with your youngster at a certain time and he is stalling the whole family. A good technique, if you can set it up in advance, is to pay a sitter to stand by at her telephone. This makes sense, particularly for the under-five child, who does not have the same social obligations as the older child. Then if he is not ready on time, leave him home! You will rarely have to repeat this rather stringent lesson.

A timer may be helpful for the dawdler. Tell him you're setting it and he must be ready when it rings. If he's not, he doesn't go. The timer has the great advantage of eliminating your voice.

When faced with dawdling, I am often reminded of Eleanor Roosevelt's response to a niece who was bewailing the fact she that hadn't had enough time to do something. "But you had all the time there was," Mrs. Roosevelt said gently.

SELFISHNESS

Three-year-old Don and three-and-a-half-year-old Carey were sitting side by side on the sofa, each with his arms crossed over his chest. Chins thrust forward, they both looked like thunderclouds.

"What is it?" asked one of the mothers.

"We are *not* sharing," said Don.

Children over three can be taught to share, when mothers work at it. But even then, as every mother knows, there are days and there are days. Before three, sharing is very tenuous. The invited child, whose toys are not in question, generally does better. The host, who may be quite amenable to sharing at other times, may embarrass his mother with "It's mine! Don't touch that!" It generally takes some effort to appease the two factions, and sometimes you have to cut a visit short. When sibling rivalry is intense, displaced feelings may be put on a visiting friend, intensifying the "Leave my territory alone" feelings. It is important to realize that selfish feelings are normal and that more kindly ones will show themselves in time. Between three and four children develop genuine relationships with others and, in doing so, learn by trial and error about the necessity to give and take. You can voice their not-so-nice feelings for them in private if you wish.

"Sometimes you like to share, but sometimes you don't. Sometimes you want *everything* for yourself."

Talk doesn't change the necessity to share, but it does keep criticism at a minimum, thereby enabling the child's more generous emotions to surface.

WHINING

One mother asked me to title this section "Cooking with Whine." She couldn't bear the querulous tones of her four-year-old as she tried to prepare the evening meal. Whining, like dawdling, is aggressive. It upsets you because it implies a hidden reproach. Since, like all mothers, you are extraordinarily responsive to even the most subtle of accusations (for the past thirty years mothers have been programmed to believe that almost everything is *their* fault), you berate yourself. Where have you failed? Why isn't your darling child satisfied?

Here the rights of mothers need to be invoked. Be blunt. "I don't like whining. Please tell me what bothers you or what it is you want." If the whining persists, send the child to his room and tell him to come back when he can talk normally. Like chalk squeaking on a blackboard, whining gets your back up. If it goes on, you get nasty—which only gives your child empirical proof of your unreasonableness. Tell him to cut it out before it gets to you. If he refuses to go to his room, pick him up bodily and put him there. If he won't stay, gate the room. Children feel safer when you mean what you say.

VERBAL ABUSE

Mothers who have encouraged their children to verbalize are often taken aback by a barrage of verbal abuse they had not anticipated.

"It's okay to tell me how you feel," says Jimmy's mother with a determinedly therapeutic gleam in her eye.

Jimmy brightens considerably. "You are a stupid dumbhead!" he shouts.

Mother, raised as she was in a more polite era, is caught off guard. She snaps, "How dare you talk to me like that!"

What happened?

Jimmy's mother mistook the use of words for genuine verbalizing. Sometimes it is the same, and sometimes it isn't. Words, when used to master a problem, as in the understanding of feelings, help the child to achieve self-control. But words can also be abusive and hurt another person. When this occurs, the child has to be shown what he is doing. "You are angry and I want to hear why," you can say, "but I don't like to be called names. It's not being nice to another person." The step from action abuse to verbal abuse, as in Jimmy's case, is a forward step in the civilizing process, but abuse is still abuse and a big mouth can be very hard to tolerate. It is a step toward genuine talking but it is *not* what I mean by verbalization, and parents do not have to be subjected to it in the name of good child rearing.

If you don't like the insults and epithets you are being subjected to, insist that these be hurled somewhere else. He can go to his room and shout imprecations. You can sit in another room and turn up the radio. It's no different from sending your child to his room when he can't manage his physical aggression. After the verbal tantrum is over, you can ask him what made him so mad. The beginning of genuine verbalizing is then a possibility. But real talk is never possible in the midst of battle, physical or otherwise. It is all right to treat verbal abuse as abuse.

MESSINESS

Hanging clothes on the floor provokes many fights between the generations. It is very hard for a mother to see how she can let a consequence follow that teaches *him* when it is *her* house which is being turned into a junk pile.

For children over four the use of a box may be helpful. Get a large box from the supermarket and place it somewhere out of sight—the basement, a spare room. Tell the kids you are not hanging up their things any more. When you find a jacket, a pair of shoes, underwear, or a scarf lying around, toss it in the box. *Eventually* they have to go to the box to redeem the article. Don't keep too many clothes around when you set this plan in motion, or your little girl may be wearing her best sleeveless party dress to a Brownie cookout in November. Have a reasonable supply of a week's clothes on hand (put out-of-season clothes in an old trunk where your child can't find them). Then watch the process work. When he wants to wear a pair of summer shorts when the snow is four feet deep, tell him you're not about to let him get pneumonia. He has to wear regular clothes. When he protests that he has none, tell him they're in the box. When he argues that his wool pants are wrinkled, tell him to hang them up the next time. As with reducing fights about mealtime, he learns by experience. Eliminating your voice helps things along. He feels you are nagging when you keep telling him what to do. You can have a rule that your child can't wear dirty clothes to school. It is his job to put his clothes in the hamper. This rule is more successful with the school-age child than with the under-five child, who is not subject to the same social pressures as his older brother or sister. When your child is between two and a half and four you will be washing his clothes almost every day, so the issue of neatness is largely your doing. However, by the time your child is three and a half or four, you can insist on his bringing his soiled clothes to the hamper. He can be asked to put clean clothing away. He can also be asked to put toys away at night. Plastic containers, clearly marked, can help the sorting process. Much of what you require in these areas is a personal matter. But you have the right to insist on *your* requirements, since your child lives in *your* house.

A college girl I know recently couldn't find her good shoes. "Did you put them in the box?" she asked her mother good-naturedly. Shades of the past!

TEMPER TANTRUMS

Temper tantrums are storms which happen when verbalization has not taken place. Your child's feelings build, but he has found no way to discharge them. His pent-up feelings have nowhere to go, and he loses control of himself in flailing, fighting, and flinging himself around.

The first thing to do with the under-five child who is besieged in this fashion is to remove him to a quiet place. It will take time for him to deaccelerate, and you want to make sure he can't hurt himself. Stay with him if he's headed in that direction. Say "I won't let you hurt yourself," as you toss pillows under him. He feels safer when you take over the controls for a short time and let him know that he can call on some of your strength to weather the storm.

If the tantrum is of a milder sort, such as stamping his foot or shouting furiously, put him in isolation and then encourage him to talk. If he is still screaming, tell him you will talk it over when he calms down. You cannot respond peaceably in the midst of a hurricane.

Getting the child to acknowledge angry feelings, important in all discipline problems, is particularly helpful with the tantrum. The best way to prevent tantrums is to allow the child to express his rage in words at the time it is felt. When anger is emitted piecemeal through words, it need not erupt into something overwhelming which frightens him as much as it does you.

Remember too that during the course of their development children will have angry feelings which are quite unrelated to your handling—as in the case of the two-year-old's negativism or the four-year-old's attempts to play one parent against the other. These are normal phases that really do pass. Often the child himself doesn't know what is eating him. If he is unable to verbalize a feeling and you cannot locate a reasonable source, tell him that he is having a bad day or that he woke up on the wrong side of bed. After all, we have our bad times too. You can sympathize with him for the tough time he's having, but you can also make it plain that he's not to take it out on other people. A reasonable premise that covers almost every situation can be summarized as follows: You can't hurt me, yourself, or the house.

Remember that fatigue or hunger can exacerbate problems. Often a good rest and a fully belly make a child more reasonable and available for talking. As with all of us, there are good and bad times for a discussion. Tact is appreciated as much by children as by adults.

FEARS

Fears are not behavioral problems, but they frequently cause problems that require parents' attention. In infancy fears of falling and of loud noises are common. In the second and third years the bathroom is sometime frightening. Children fear being pulled down the drain or even being flushed away in the toilet. Since a two-year-old's perceptions of size differences are all askew, he doesn't know he is too big for the drain and may clutch frantically at his mother's knee in an attempt to avoid being put in the bathtub. The same youngster may fling himself unconcernedly into the swimming pool. Fears of vacuum cleaners, sirens, thunder, lightning, spiders, and bees are common and tend to come and go as young children perceive and misperceive the realities around them.

Parents who understand immature thinking take these fears seriously. Comfort and console your child, then explain the facts as they really are. "You can't go down the drain." If he clutches harder, you may have to add, "You're too big."

If he is still unconvinced, tell him, "I won't let you."

Sponge bathing a child who suffers from such distorted views is not spoiling him. The fear will pass soon enough— and then you won't be able to get him out of the tub.

What if he fears imaginary intruders? Night lights can help dispel them. Dogs, which children generally regard as four-legged people, are sometimes perceived as jungle preda- tors. The child's emotional state can color the most benign objects with fright and horror. You hold to the realities. "The dog is just yawning. He doesn't want to bite." If he is frightened by dog in the street, tell him, "The dog is on a chain. I won't let him bite you." Once again you are the voice of reality and the protector.

Fear of body damage comes up over and over again with each successive year of development. He needs reassurance. "No, your nose will not break off. The ashtray which broke is not like a part of you. People don't break."

Television programs can make for upsets. In some shows, arms disappear, people are decapitated, people are eaten, witches seem real. It helps to keep an eye on what your children are watching because these programs, though pre- sumably designed for children, often contribute to unneces- sary fears. Fairytales too can be very gory, but their effect on the child is moderated by the teller.

With TV, you may be able to quiet fears by telling him, "It's only pretend." If this doesn't allay his fear, teach him to turn the set off by himself. "You don't need to see that scary program. Let's turn it off." The active shutting away of TV monsters can relieve his sense of helplessness. The knowledge that fears are normal and that they will pass should help you endure your child's inappropriate response.

Nightmares can disturb even young children. Their imma- ture emotional equipment creates distortions which can wake them in a fright. Here too comfort is best. "It's not real; it's a dream" can pin a name to an unnamable dread. Some- times you need to sit with them at night until these dissipate.

Greater maturity helps them cope better, but nightmares will surface from time to time for the rest of their lives.

Finally, let's not forget that children need privacy. They don't have to tell us everything they do or feel. They work out many of their problems by themselves in the course of growing up. The recommendations I have made in this chapter are designed to help provide a sensible framework for a child's life. They are intended not to interfere with normal growth and development but rather to be of background assistance.

V

Sex Education

Ever since your child was conceived, you thought about how you would one day tell him how he came to be. You don't plan to repeat your parents' mistakes by hushing it up. You don't want him to think sex is dirty. You don't want him to rely on street information—or, more likely, misinformation. You want, in short, to do it right.

Cheer up. It's not that hard. What makes it seem so difficult is the fact that sex is a highly charged subject, even for the most liberated among us. We may know the end result we'd like to achieve—namely, children who accept themselves and their bodies and grow up to be the kinds of people who are able to have meaningful human relationships. But how to get there is the question.

As with other topics I've discussed, the educational process is gradual. Sex education requires that a child be aware of himself as a human being with ties to others, for no one conceives himself or develops independently of others. Man differs from many other species in this regard; he has a very long childhood in terms of being dependent on his parents for years. The child's knowledge of himself as a boy (or of herself as a girl) develops in the early years. Sex education involves helping the child to establish himself as a person and to build his capacity for mature relationships with others. It is not just teaching him the facts about where babies come from. If we tend to talk about birds or bees or pollen and get mystical about nature with our children, it is because this topic makes us nervous. Our zeal to align ourselves with other animals is proportionate, I think, to our anxiety.

SEX EDUCATION IS LIFE EDUCATION

Sex education is really life education, and you have already done a good deal of it by the time your child is three years old. Whether or not you have used the methods in this book, you have done many things which helped establish your child as an individual. When you held him for feedings, when you walked him during illness, when you played peekaboo with him and enjoyed him in his bath, you were helping him take pleasure in you and in himself. His affection for you and yours for him build the very first tie in his young life. He loves Mommy in the beginning. His clinging and crying between eight and fourteen months is his way of saying he loves you. In effect, he says to strangers, "You are not Mommy, so get lost!" He is becoming selective in his choices; his ability to discriminate among adults who take care of him shows his increasing good sense. His preference for one person is a feature of loyalty. His undivided love for you helps build the ability to love the others who will eventually follow.

Toilet training, which all children eventually must undergo, contributes to body mastery and enhances the sense of self. While the methods recommended in this book increase the latter, it is also true that all children achieve cleanliness in time. This, plus disciplinary measures which help children achieve better self-control, are part and parcel of self-mastery, which is a natural precursor to relating to others. How much better you can like other people if you like yourself! Children like themselves better when they function well.

Teaching a child to be considerate is an important factor in sex education. When a father shares in some of the tasks of caring for house and children, a child learns a lot about how men and women relate to each other. Such gestures can demonstrate respect and add to a girl's pride in herself as a female and to a boy's understanding that a man can be sensitive and caring. It isn't only what you say. It's what you do. The parents' unity, often difficult to attain, particularly in the early years of marriage, is the best sex education of all.

Try to stand together on most things regarding child rearing, if you possibly can. Talking together at night can iron out a lot of differences. Most parents don't think of themselves as educators; but once they do and once they recognize how important it is for their children to see them in agreement, they find that, in matters of discipline especially, the effort is worthwhile. On the other hand, some differences are unavoidable. But from these children learn another important fact: the world doesn't collapse because loved ones are angry with each other. Making up and forgiveness are part of living together. In this sense, sex education is a continuing part of your family life.

THE NEW SEXUAL FREEDOM

But the aspect of sex education that concerns modern parents most is how to make children comfortable with and unashamed of their own sexuality. The feeling among many parents these days is that what is natural should be accepted as natural. No one should feel guilty about normal body functions. The assumption here is that if these are accepted calmly from the beginning of life, the child will not regard them as dirty or as matters to be hidden. There is the conviction that one doesn't hide one's body; it too is a natural phenomenon.

This approach assumes that input from the environment is the most significant factor in sex education. In effect, modern parents are saying, "See, we are not embarrassed. All is open here. You can see for yourself what sex differences are like." They assume that seeing is believing and, therefore, comprehending. The hope is that children, after seeing their parents and each other undressed, will ask questions which can then be answered directly, without evasion. Then guilt, thought to have been inspired by the attitudes of a sexually inhibited society, will be eliminated. There is the hope that a better man will emerge from such honesty.

This type of thinking has developed as a reaction to the rigid, secretive view of sex held in the Victorian era, when sex was equated with original sin and repression was the order of the day. The modern recognition that all people have sexual feelings and that such feelings are normal is a significant one. Proponents of the new freedom have gone further, however, concluding that man will accept his body functions with less self-consciousness if he is not constrained by a modesty which implies that enjoyment of physical pleasure should be hidden.

THE BOOMERANG

The curious thing is that this thinking, which seems logical enough, has boomeranged in ways not anticipated by its advocates. Observers of young children who were raised with this new, open approach to sexuality found, much to their dismay, that the children were not freer because of this new freedom but instead were more excitable and often less educable. There was a great deal of guilt which could not be explained. This happened because in the new freedom, which put great weight on parental and societal attitudes toward sex, the factor of infantile sexuality was not understood.

What we have learned through the close observation of young children over many years is that there are precursors to adult sexuality. Even very little children enjoy body excitements. They suck their thumbs or touch their genitals. Today this is viewed as normal, acceptable human behavior.

That such behavior evokes anxiety in us is not so surprising when we consider that a normal forgetting occurs in all of us at age five or six. Repression sets in about then and we can't remember much, if any, of our own early histories. That is one reason for the general disbelief that greets these theories.

A long biological and emotional process starts when the child is born. In his early years the child has to contend with the physical excitements that erupt from time to time in normal development. What the proponents of the new freedom did not understand was that the child has his own feelings about body excitement. They were surprised to learn that these feelings lead to guilt spontaneously. Parental openness and nudity, rather than ridding the child of these feelings, frequently make for more inner conflicts. What we have learned in the study of young children is that it does not help the child to be put in the passive position of viewer. Exposure to adult nudity, with its size discrepancies, can be too much for the child when he is contending with dimly understood drives of his own. It is not a moral issue; rather it is one of overloading the circuit. It raises far more questions than it answers and mixes him up far more than straight talk which answers his questions.

A PRACTICAL APPROACH

This does not mean that I recommend a return to Victorian secretiveness and denial of sexuality. That period brought a suffocating air of hypocrisy to normal life. Instead, I recommend that you talk to your child about what he wants to know. Talk is better than a demonstration, and it is essential to make sex a permissible topic for discussion. In that way, you avoid the pitfalls of the hush-hush school of thought as much as the problems of the exhibitionist school of thought.

Now, to be more specific. I recommend from the first, if possible (certainly by three months), having the child sleep in a separate bedroom. Even keeping his crib in your bedroom during the day (if space is limited) and rolling it into the living room at night is advantageous, because it announces firmly that sleep is sleep and that you and he both need some privacy in which to effect it. This avoids a lot of sleep problems later on and is worth the extra discomfort of making special arrangements. If there are older children who will be disturbed, it is still better, in the long run, that the baby share a room with them rather than with you.

I make a special point of this because the sexual aspect of adult relationships is something that the child should not be permitted to see. Such observations, instead of teaching him the facts, overwhelm him. You may be surprised to learn that very small babies are aware of what is going on in the other bed. Certainly they don't understand what is happening, but just as certainly they are aware that something is. Since infants can't tell us their thoughts, we only learn of their confusions retrospectively, and what we have learned is that small minds misperceive and are needlessly frightened. They take two and two and make seven.

"He is trying to kill her with a knife," Stevie, four, told me soberly. "He hits her and hits her and hits her!" When I asked why he didn't tell his parents how he felt, he answered, "But then he'll kill me." The parents had assured me he had never observed them. "He's a sound sleeper," they said.

One couple was horrified to see three-year-old Elizabeth next to their bed at night. "What are you doing to my Mommy?" she asked indignantly of her father.

There is nothing in the child's experience to explain what is happening in the other bed. He interprets what he sees in the light of his poorly developed comprehension. It stirs him up in ways he finds hard to handle.

This recommendation for privacy includes other areas as well—dressing, undressing, and toileting. You may be bewildered about this because so much of what you read advises otherwise. Further, you may wonder how you can follow this recommendation in the face of one bathroom and little ones tumbling over themselves to be near Mommy.

It is easier to do if you are first clear about the reasons. The major reason is that your child's mind is not able to take in realistically what he sees. He indulges in a kind of fairytale thinking at this stage of his life. Size differences loom as enormous.

"My father's pee-pee is one hundred feet long," Michael, three, announced to me sadly. His sense of proportion was quite absurd, but his outstretched arms, as he tried to show me the size, told me how he *felt* looking at his father—outclassed and inadequate. Even if a child doesn't voice his response, and most do not, it can leave him feeling unnecessarily "lesser than."

LEARNING FROM PEERS

Feelings are attached to observations, and little ones do better when they learn about sex differences from their own age group. Size differences are then less of an issue. Even then, children under five have their difficulties. They assume, in the egocentricity of babyhood, that everyone is made as they are. When they are confronted with the reality of difference, little minds go to work and derive many elaborate, if false, conclusions.

"What happened to her wee-wee?" asked Johnny about a new baby sister. "If it can happen to her," Johnny added ominously, "it can happen to me." He barricaded his bed at night with every toy he could find, defending against a threat that was all in his head.

Amy, three, asked her mother matter of factly to put the penis on her Christmas list. "It's so handy for standing up," she said. She was very disappointed when she opened her packages that year.

This kind of "Anything I wish, I can make happen" thinking is very marked in the toddler. Here wishes come true, body parts vanish, and spiders eat little children. Avoiding exposure to the giants of his world eliminates a sizable hunk of unnecessary anxiety. By keeping your bathroom and bedroom door shut, you give the child a chance to cope, on his own terms, with his own biology. He doesn't have to deal with the stimulation that comes from viewing yours. He will still need to contend with the normal worries of his age, but they will not be so overpowering. And, as he grows older, his ability to understand will grow accordingly. Time is on your side.

Don't hesitate to answer if your child protests your shutting the door. "I want my privacy," you can say. Very soon he will demand the same for himself. "If you have questions, I'll answer them," you can add.

THE IMPORTANCE OF HONESTY

Your best bet in dealing with children's misconceptions is to be honest and to the point. Asking him what he has heard or thinks is a great help because then you can try to straighten out his distortions. It also gives you time to think of an appropriate answer. So ask him, "What do you think? What have you heard?"

You can tell Johnny that nothing has happened to his sister's wee-wee. Girls are made differently from boys. She does not have one like his but that is the way she is supposed to be. If you hear him make a remark that reveals a misconception, straighten him out on the spot; little children seem to require this. Each round with you, he learns a little more, and you don't have to do it all in one day. His intelligence is growing; a greater awareness is possible.

To childish minds, something visible is seen as a plus; something not seen is felt to be a minus. Both sexes struggle with the problem of difference and need repeated clarification. Michael needs to be told his fears are needless; Amy needs to know that she has something too, but it can't be seen. It delights her to learn that she can have babies when she grows up. You can acknowledge that it's hard to wait till then. Two-to-three-year-olds, being in the "who's got what" stage of development, are inordinately curious, but this passes in time. It is succeeded by the "I want what the other fellow has" stage.

Eric, three and a half, walked around with a peculiar gait as he stuck his stomach out ahead of him. "I can *too* have a baby," he stoutly maintained.

Little girls wish to be little boys; little boys wish to be little girls. They all wish they could be grownups and stay up later. It's a normal human belief that the grass on the other side is greener. In children's play we see a lot of switching back and forth; boys play with dolls, girls want to be daddies, and everyone likes to be boss. Mother wonders, as she hears her officious four-year-old telling off some younger playmate, whether she herself really sounds like that.

One of the nicest things about children's play is that it allows them to take any part they choose. They can always meet reality later with "It's only a game." But for the period of the play, children get a chance to express many wishes and ideas. You needn't interfere with ordinary play by stopping it and educating them. Play has educational and therapeutic advantages in itself. It is one of the means by which children learn to cope, and its variety and make-believe elements help children endure the painful swings of childhood. In play, they can make things come out as they wish.

PLAYING "DOCTOR"

However, when children want to examine each other or exhibit to each other, they should be stopped. This may seem like unnecessary adult interference to you, but "doctor" games and the like are not helpful to children because they are too stimulating. They can interfere with sleep, with quiet times, and with ordinary play. You can say, "I don't want you to play that. It's too exciting for you." Don't be afraid to break up group activities of this kind. You can say to them, "That's enough. It stirs you up too much." Children are relieved when adults stop them, even though they may protest vehemently. If you insist on modesty for yourself, they will be less inclined to play these games and their interest in them will diminish.

THE BENEFITS OF MODESTY

Many modern parents have been used to undressing and dressing in front of their children. This does not mean that it is too late to make changes in the direction of more modesty; at any point you begin, your child will benefit.

David, five, was brought to me because of his out-of-control fighting in kindergarten. As I talked with him about what he thought his problem was all about, he announced, "I play nudies with my sister."

I asked, "And how do you do that?" To which he replied, "First we take off all our clothes except for our undershirts and underpants."

"And then what do you do?"

"Oh, and then we take those off." David's out-of-control behavior in school stemmed from his parents' genuine efforts to be modern and open about their bodies. When modesty was instituted, his behavior in school improved proportionately. Though not all out-of-control behavior has this source, reducing stimulation in the home decreases the chances of it.

CHANGE GRADUALLY

If you've let your kids wander in and out of the bathroom and bedroom at will, don't change your system abruptly. A sudden change in the rules may arouse more questions than it answers. If you see the point of this recommendation and are willing to go along with it, get into the change slowly. You might gradually introduce the idea of privacy and tell the children you prefer it. In a month or so they will probably be requesting it for themselves. If you feel you can't leave toddlers around to commit mayhem while you are in the bathroom, tie the baby to his dressing table and have the toddler wait on the couch or in the old playpen until you reappear. It may seem like an unnecessary to-do over a small matter, but the point is that it is not a small matter to them. They will stop trying to get into the bathroom after a week or so. If a child barges in unexpectedly, keep covered and tell him to leave. He'll catch on.

If you worry about his locking himself in, remove the bathroom lock and put up hooks both inside and outside near the top of the door to ensure privacy for yourself. He loves it when you respect his wish for privacy too, as when you knock before you enter. Obviously, with little ones who are toilet training, you will be in on their privacy for at least part of the training interval. Nevertheless, your requesting privacy for yourself sets a tone which is calming.

Sometimes parents are confused by the fact that their children appear not to notice nudity and seem to take it in stride very well. There is no doubt that some children manage better than others, as some have a greater tolerance for excitement. But many children who seem overly aggressive are frequently working off sexual steam. Often this is not recognized by innocent parents such as David's.

You may feel that my suggestions smack of prudery and that children will become peeping Toms if their view is blocked. This will not happen if you are frank in fulfilling their need for information. Their curiosity is real and needs an outlet. If they do play doctor, ask what it is they want to know. As in other areas of child rearing, such as discipline, you are saying "no" to the acting out of the curiosity and "yes" to the request for information.

BATHING TOGETHER

After they are two, I would begin to discourage the children's being bathed together. This too can roil them up and is really unnecessary. The easiest system starts the privacy early. It doesn't mean becoming shocked and outraged if you find them looking or touching. It does mean stopping the activity in a firm way and then opening the way for talk. Recognize with them that they are curious and thereby show your willingness to respond to questions. This helps demonstrate your credibility and honesty. Later, when they have more pressing questions, it helps them to know they can turn to you. If separate baths are too much work for you, try bathing one child one night and another the next.

THE OEDIPUS COMPLEX

After the "I want what he or she has" phase, young children may show intense feelings of affection for various members of their immediate family. Between three and a half and five, little boys want to marry their mothers, little girls their fathers. Sometimes boys wants to marry their daddies and girls their mommies. They may love older siblings with an adoration that is quite unwarranted, since the sibling in question may pay absolutely no attention to this unsolicited hero worship.

A college student said to me, on hearing theories about the Oedipus complex in his psychology class, "You don't have to do anything about it, right?"

Right.

The processes frequently go on silently, and you may never see or hear any of this. It isn't necessary that you do. Some children are more verbal than others; each child has his own style. The important thing is that you function as Mommy for them and that's real and safe. You are not actually a beautiful princess even though your son, at age four, may think you are. When four-year-old Lisa tells her mother, "I want to marry Daddy," mother shouldn't feel offended or go into a long discourse on sex choices.

She can say matter of factly, "He's already married. You can't."

If Lisa then spends a year or two struggling with her frustration over this unavoidable fact, that's the way the process goes. Learning about reality takes time. There is bound to be frustration along the way. If mother realizes that in a few years Lisa will want to do everything her mother does, she need not feel hurt by a preference her daughter is now so candid about. If mother wants to, she can sympathize with the feeling. "It's hard to wait until you get your own husband." Sometimes a child's anger at her mother is a reflection of this normal phase of development. You don't have to get tense about it. Sometimes a child is irritable with one parent or the other for weeks, perhaps months, at a time. He may be going through such a phase.

One mother was always charming in her manner toward her four-year-old daughter.

"Good morning!" she said brightly as she entered her daughter's bedroom.

"It's not good!" said Margo balefully.

Mother threw open the curtains. "What a lovely day!" she continued in a vehemently cheerful tone.

"I hate it!" said Margo.

Mother felt like a failure. What had she done to deserve this? Not a thing. Her daughter was going through what might be called a developmental disease. She was Oedipal in her attachments; mother was her rival. Nothing mother could do would please her.

Once you realize that these feelings lie within the child and that they are transitory, you will be able to be more matter of fact and less hurt. When you know that it is her problem, you don't make it yours by trying harder to please her. You ignore some of her testing provocations, knowing that change for the better will come—eventually. She may want to fight about choice of clothes or other minutiae. These are transitory issues that you needn't get too involved in. They are times to be endured, and a rueful acceptance of a "You can't win" philosophy can help you survive.

FEARS AND GUILT GO TOGETHER

Some childhood fears have their roots in this period of emotional turmoil. Here again, matter-of-fact reality is best. "No, there is no monster in the room. Yes, you may have a night light if you want it."

These fears too almost always pass. When the fears seem overwhelming and do not respond to common-sense reassurance, it is frequently because openness in the home, often done with the best intent, has increased the child's normal sexual feelings and hence his guilt. For guilt, contrary to the ideas of many, comes primarily from within. If Larry wants to get rid of his father so he can marry his mother, he feels very guilty because he loves his father too. No wonder monsters are out to get him.

COOLING IT

The best way to deal with all of this is to cool it. Modesty, privacy, and less roughhousing are all helpful. Try to separate the sexes, however difficult it may be. If a boy and girl must sleep in the same room, you can put up a screen between beds; even a blanket on a line will do. The children may circumvent you occasionally, but do send each back to his own side. By requiring privacy for yourself and expecting your children to respect the need for it among themselves, you let them know where you stand. Even if they evade you occasionally, it's a comfort for them to know you prefer less excitement, not more. It relieves them in the same way that all good disciplining does—by letting them know that someone will stop them from behaving inappropriately.

Dennis, four, was brought to me because he was always hurting himself. His legs were crisscrossed with scars from old injuries. "If there is one pebble in the road, he will trip on it and skin his knee," said his mother. This active and demonstrably well-coordinated little boy was endlessly falling, bumping, and jarring himself. He whimpered over small bruises which he inflicted on himself.

When I asked him about these, he whispered, "I want to get hurt." Later I learned he thought he *deserved* to get hurt. Nudity in his home had stirred him up sexually and he thought he was wicked for his thoughts and his wishes. The parents helped him a lot by keeping their clothes on and not stimulating him further. It was gratifying to see him decrease his self-injuries as his newly developing conscience tormented him less. He had less need to punish himself so aggressively.

BED PROBLEMS

If you're short on space you may have to stagger bedtimes to maintain any privacy at all. Putting one child to bed in your room and then moving him later eliminates a lot of bedtime hijinks. It is best, if you can manage it, to have boys share one room and girls share another.

Letting children into the parents' bed in the morning is a common family custom that everyone enjoys. But it too may lead to unnecessary wildness. One mother I know who slept in the nude used to take her children into bed with her on Sunday mornings. One day her son, as he stood at the door, handed her a robe. "Is he telling me something?" she asked.

If Sunday morning pile-ins are too pleasant a family treat to give up, have the children play with toys on the floor near you or at the foot of your bed on top of the blankets. The cuddling which you enjoy in a maternal way may be misconstrued by the child when he's passing through a normal competitive phase at four or so. Please understand that I am not against all parental demonstrations of love and affection; they are as important to a child's development as the sun is to flowers. But warmth need not mean kisses on the mouth, and a cuddle need not mean breast fondling. Parental affection need not be seductive.

TOILET TRAINING

Toilet training is a period where children often do a great deal of observing of each other. This is far better than observing adults, and I wouldn't make an issue of it. They can be allowed to talk about the differences as they observe them. If they seem to get too excited by such observations, tell them so and separate them. When they are two and a half or three, you can press the need for privacy. Children often seem pleased with the idea of closing doors.

MASTURBATION

The calming environment you aim for should lessen a lot of infantile behavior. Masturbation in either sex may occur for a time; it is normal but it may need management if it becomes public. Tell your child that touching himself is a private matter. It doesn't belong in the living room. This acknowledges, in effect, that it goes on but defines it realistically as a private matter. No amount of saying "no" to a child about masturbation stops it anyhow. It is he who has to struggle with his thoughts about the rightness or wrongness of it, and he does better when we allow it to be his private business. The reason masturbation may become a kind of moral issue for *him* is *not* that we threaten him (days of predicting his genitals will fall off or that he will become an imbecile are gone forever, I hope). It may become one because, during the Oedipal phase, masturbation gets connected with sexual fantasies about parents. It may make you

feel uncomfortable to think that your child may be having
sexual thoughts about you (and since children rarely voice
these thoughts, you may find it doubly hard to believe). Just
remember: sexual interest is normal and generally silent, and
you don't have to do anything about it.

SEXUAL INTEREST DECLINES IN
SIX-TO-TEN-YEAR-OLDS

At five and six the child becomes far more interested in
others. Teachers become persons to admire; often parents
count for less. The schoolchild turns more and more to
friends and to learning outside the home, and others enrich
his life as his world is enlarged. For a period of time his
sexual interests become dormant. The elementary school
child may show a casual interest in the opposite sex at times,
but for the most part boys are busy playing with boys and
girls prefer to play with girls.

This is the time of life when curiosity about the real world
is at a peak. Children are eager to learn. They enjoy groups
of various sorts and organize clubs of their own. These dis-
band with great rapidity and new ones take their place.
School-age children have private lives in which friends and
secret exchanges are especially important. Camping may be
a new interest for both sexes; collecting various kinds of
objects can become a mania for a time. Music lessons, danc-
ing classes, scouts, and a multitude of other special interests
claim their attention. Your problem as the parent of an
elementary school child may be to keep some free time open
for him. For too many children of this age, the waking hours
are overorganized. They need time to let their motors idle.

Questions about sexual matters come up occasionally in
six-to-ten-year-olds but in a more perfunctory and academic
way than they did when the children were under five and
struggling for control. In a real sense, the subject gets easier.
They have words to converse with, and they hear you in a

new way. While they turn to friends for information (or misinformation), the fact that you have leveled with them all along makes them better able to judge and weigh what they hear realistically.

- don't avoid questions
- privacy

VI
More about
Sex Education

Mark Twain's joke about the weather could be applied in reverse to the sex education of children: "Everybody does something about it but nobody talks about it." To which I would add, "And when they do, it generally mixes the children up even more." That is because no one really helped us to understand when we were young, and we find ourselves tongue-tied as we try to explain emotions and experiences that are really nonverbal in nature. Feelings of a very profound sort are involved. There is passion in sex and we have known and felt it in a wordless way. The attempt to use words throws us off. We feel awkward in our attempts to explain.

AVOIDING THE PITFALLS

So sometimes we lie. "The doctor brings the baby." We cheer ourselves up with the thought that it is a little lie. After all, the doctor *helps* bring the baby.

Or we postpone. "You'll understand better when you're older." There! That gets him off our back for now.

Or we get intellectual. We produce elaborate charts and drawings to explain reproduction. This is far beyond him, but if the experts say it's important to tell a child about sex, why tell we will! This could be called a compliance dodge. We tell the facts, but in such a way that he can't understand them.

Or we get immodest. We hope he will understand about sex differences by seeing us undressed. But nudity doesn't really present the facts. An unseen vagina is a fact, but a child wouldn't know about it by looking. What nudity *does* do is effectively stop communication. Children who have seen a lot generally do not ask questions. They are too mixed up to know where to begin. Adult exposure generally withers discussion as effectively as charts and graphs. It is another way of saying, "Look, but don't ask." Further, it presents the child with a real dilemma, for he has no way to discharge his own sexual tension.

Or we get poetic. "It's beautiful when people love." The child presses for more information than mother would like to give. But she's been told to be truthful so she takes the plunge. "It's like kissing," she says bravely. "The Daddy puts the penis in the Mommy's vagina when they want to have a baby."

"I think that's disgusting," says four-year-old Peggy. Her idea of the genitals is connected to bathroom activity.

"You must have done it three times," says Ted, counting on his kindergarten fingers.

"Wait till I tell Craig," yells Tommy. "He thinks you get babies at the hospital."

No wonder parents hope schools will do the job. Or the clergy. Or anybody else.

STRAIGHT TALK IS BEST

Is there any way we can go about educating children in a practical fashion that avoids these pitfalls? If stretching the truth, postponing, sidestepping, demonstrating, and intellectualizing don't teach, what will?

Talking will. But it is talking of a very special kind. It is talk that relates to the thinking process of a particular age. It is not just giving the facts.

Knowing when and how much information to give is important because sexuality begins at a very early age. In fact, it begins far earlier than most of us would suppose. A normal forgetting sets in at age five or so, and none of us can remember these early feelings in ourselves. We begin to believe in infantile sexuality only because we see and hear it in our children.

There are three steps which are helpful in the sex education of the young.

The first is modesty.

David, the child in the last chapter who was excited by the "nudies" game he played with his sister, had many pleasures taken away from him as his mother worked with me over a period of time. She stopped the games; she closed all doors; she had his grandmother read stories to him on the couch, instead of lying down with him at night. One day as they were sitting at a table together, she asked him how he felt about these changes she had made.

He put his elbow on the table and pointed a finger at her. "Listen," he said, shaking it for emphasis, "anything Mrs. Weisberger tells you to do, you do it." He appreciated his new ability to be calmer and to pay better attention in school. He felt it was worth the sacrifice of infantile pleasures. In a human way, he showed a regret or two. A year after our work together, David's mother told him she was going to see me. Did he have a message? He was thoughtful. "Yes," he said. "You can tell her that I don't do it any more. But sometimes I would still *like* to play nudies." The transition from the pleasure principle to the reality principle is not easy for anyone at any age.

The second step is talk. Talking provides the channel by which we educate. When you talk to your child about issues which concern him, you are heard better. You can then concentrate on correcting his mixed-up perceptions.

The beginning phase of verbalized sex education directs itself to the first major issue which confronts young children —the issue of sexual differences. This is what concerns the child at about age two, and this is what requires explanation. Very understandably, he assumes that everyone is made like himself. It is quite a shock to discover others are made differently. So, somewhere between age two and three, you must help him to slowly recognize that everyone is made as he or she is supposed to be. The children he sees are intact, and so is he. His understanding of this is important in building self-acceptance. His self-esteem may then proceed normally. It may take quite a while before he fully accepts this recognition of difference. His limited ability to comprehend what he sees often conflicts with stories he concocts to explain what is not a very simple matter to his small brain. Your main task at this early time is to ask what he thinks. Try not to laugh at his speculations. Then set him straight.

Arthur, two, put small toy trucks in his swimming trunks at the YMCA swimming classes he attended with his mother. He kept shouting "Boke!" Then he ran home, stripped his clothes off, refused to put them back on, and strutted around with a belligerent air.

This strange behavior continued for some time. Then his mother suddenly realized "boke" meant "broke" and his concerns were for the ladies he saw undressed who were not endowed as he was. The trucks in the swimsuit were to protect his vital member. The strutting said, "See, I'm intact. I'm really okay. Not 'boke' at all."

Once Arthur's mother realized that he was in the normal "who's got what" stage, his strange behavior became understandable. She could then reassure him. She even went further and dressed him for swimming at home, bypassing the locker room, so as not to encounter the adult nudity the swimming pool fostered.

CLEARING UP CONFUSION

In this phase you tell them boys have a penis. Girls have a vagina. It is a tube which is inside. You can't see it but it is there. All people were born the way they were supposed to be. Half the people in the world are girls and women; half are men and boys. No one changes from one to the other. Both sexes are important and parts are made as they are supposed to be. Try to do this slowly, over a period of time. Let your explanations come in response to questions.

You try not to laugh as their wish for magic overrides their good sense. They go back to early notions even after you've clarified the realities. This is a rumination which helps them digest their new knowledge. You may wonder why I stress the importance of clarifying mixups when children often persist in repeating misinformation even after you've explained things. It is because the process of being set straight, though requiring repetition, takes much of the fear and tension out of normal mental mixups at the time when distortions are most likely to occur. It's a bit like digging up new soil for a growing garden but recognizing that you have to weed as you go.

The third step is additional enlightenment. This means talking as you have already done but with an extra tuning into what your child is telling you. It is a dialogue which recognizes that the child has grown in his ability to understand. This is possible somewhere between the ages of three and five. (It can start earlier and go later, depending on the child's ability to verbalize and the questions he is struggling with.)

EARLY QUESTIONS

The child's first questions often relate to pregnancy. That is, after all, a highly visible process.

Here again, try to make your response part of a genuine

dialogue if you can. Ask him what he's heard or what he thinks of the big tummy he sees. This enables two helpful things to happen:

1. It gives you time to collect your wits and to figure out what you think!
2. It enables you to educate in a way which is more to the point.

All he really needs to hear at this time is that the baby grows in a special place near Mommy's tummy but not in it. You can give it a name—womb or uterus—if he asks for it. Sometimes he mixes it up and talks about the lady swallowing something. You correct him. "No, it's not *in* the tummy. It's *near* the tummy."

You may find that he persists in his confusion as you hear him repeat his error six months or a year later. This is because the young child's view of the entrances and exits of the body is fairly primitive. Just tell him again. The simplest explanation is the best, especially when it's in response to a question he has.

The next question may be, "Where did I come from?"

Answer: "You grew inside of Mommy."

He may notice pregnant women or animals. You can talk about everybody in the world having a Mommy. You explain that dog mommies make puppies and cat mommies make kittens. Each animal makes a baby like itself.

"But how did I start? How did I get in there?"

You can tell him about a tiny egg which the Mommy's body makes. You can relate the process to other living things. When he wants to know how the baby grows inside, tell him about the cozy place the baby rests in. He is fed by a cord which gives the baby food until he or she is ready to come out. It takes nine months before a baby is ready. The baby needs that time to grow from a tiny egg into a real person.

LATER QUESTIONS

This may be all that is necessary for some time. Later new questions may come.

"Where does the baby come out?"

You counter with your question, "What do you think?"

"I think the Daddy cuts the Mommy open with a knife," said Jennifer.

"No," said Robby. "The doctor does it."

"No," you answer. "When the baby is ready to come out, it starts pushing. It pushes out of the place it's been growing, into a tube called the vagina. That's the inside tube girls and ladies have. It pushes out of this tube head first. When it comes out, that is when we say a baby is born."

"But you said the vagina is near the wee-wee and BM place," worries Nancy, five. "How can a baby come out of such a tiny place?"

"It stretches," you reply, "like a rubber band."

"Did that happen to me?" she asks.

"Yes, and to everybody else."

"Well, maybe to everybody else," says five-year-old Allen, "but not to me." Denial of what they hear is very common. Don't worry about it. It's part of the yes-no process of absorption.

The next question may concern what part the father plays. This is generally the most difficult topic to discuss. But at some point—perhaps when the child is four or five (perhaps somewhat later)—he will want to know.

"I know about you," said Beth to her mother. "You borned me. But what about Daddy? Why is he my Daddy? How did he get to be a Daddy anyhow?"

This questioning may be more direct than what most of us hear. But in some form or other the question *does* come.

Beth's mother seized her opportunity.

"It takes two people to make a baby. A Daddy and a Mommy. The Daddy's body makes something called sperm;

the Mommy's body makes the egg. When the egg and the sperm meet, that is the beginning of a baby."

THE BIG QUESTION

That is often sufficient for some time. You don't want to overwhelm a child with information before he requests it. When he finally asks how the sperm you've told him about meets the egg you've told him about, you are faced with The Question. Often it comes in the school-age years, but by this time you've already done a good part of the educating. This preliminary talking makes the description of intercourse not as difficult a task as you had thought.

You can tell your child that when a Mommy and Daddy love each other they want to hug each other. They sleep together and when they love, the sperm comes out of the Daddy's penis and enters the Mommy's vagina, where it meets the egg that the Mommy's body has made. This is called fertilizing. When an egg is fertilized, it is the beginning of a baby.

Your child might not react at all to this information. Yet it is still worthwhile to have answered him. Honesty builds a relationship which provides a channel for future communication. It tells him that when he talks to you, you don't turn him off.

OTHER AIDS

If he wants more information than you can offer, don't hesitate to use a book. This is also helpful for the nonverbal child who doesn't ask questions at all. In the latter case, leave the book around when he shows interest, or leave it around to elicit interest. That is better than plunging in when he hasn't asked. You can read the book to him. I particularly like *The Wonderful Story of How You Were Born* (Doubleday, 1970) by Sidonie Matsner Gruenberg because it is simply written and acknowledges the feeling side as well as the factual side of conception. Some of the phraseology I have used here comes from that book. Who says finding the words is easy? Another fine book is *How New Life Begins* (Follett, 1969) by Esther K. Meeks and Elizabeth Bagwell.

If necessary, you can draw pictures. (You may need a book yourself to remember how the Fallopian tubes look.) This goes along with the modesty I've recommended. Children aren't allowed to see you nude because that neither clarifies their thinking nor neutralizes their excitement. Talk and more talk, books, and pictures do the job better because they explain things calmly and accurately.

If your child catches you at an inappropriate time for explanations—such as when you're on your way to a wedding and his piping voice asks, "When is the baby coming?" or when your very proper mother-in-law is visiting and he asks you when he is going to make sperm like Daddy—stop him. Tell him these are private matters and not to be talked about with other people. Tell him you will explain what he wants to know later. But be sure to get back to him. Here again, your reliability is underscored. Children are generally tactful about this when you educate them as to what is socially appropriate and what is not.

MODESTY AGAIN

A last word on the issue of modesty. It can present small but annoying problems for parents. I think it is worth the effort to achieve it because the more you comprehend the risk, the more you do to minimize it. With a large family, the organizing of who goes into the bathroom when may require some supervision. The kitchen sink may be used for extra washups when congestion gets bad. If young children can't wait to be toileted, try to be clothed yourself when they do come in. Insist on a closed door for yourself.

Outside the home, the difficulties are greater. Some men's

rooms do not have doors on the stalls. If you must use one of these, try to shield the child by blocking entrance to the toilet he is using. You can give him some privacy by facing in the other direction, and you can observe it yourself by asking him to turn around. Open urinals for men make for unnecessary confrontations, so try to toilet ahead to avoid these. Bathrooms in most gas stations can be used if an emergency requires a stop. In general, gas stations are more private and present a desirable alternative to public facilities.

Modesty is not easy to achieve in an era where swimming pools, restaurants, school lockers, and campsites fail to provide for privacy in dressing and toileting. Public facilities often separate the sexes, but they do not separate adults from children. If your child does observe the genitals of other adults, comment on the fact that you noticed him observing these grownups. You can ask him if he has any questions about what he's seen. One four-year-old said, "That man's pee-pee looked like a waterfall!" Some parents have disagreed with me, suggesting that I favor a modesty which only makes kids wonder what the adults are hiding. Sometimes they draw an analogy to primitive tribes and suggest that nudity makes for fewer adult sexual hangups. This is a false comparison. Your child will be growing up in a very different and complicated world, one that requires self-control and that values privacy. The young child demonstrates his pleasure in privacy particularly when parents yield him the same right of closed doors that they require for themselves.

Nursery school teachers often toilet young children together in the belief that this will help the children accept sexual differences without being troubled by discrepancy in size. There are arguments to be made on both sides of the question. Even at home, some parents feel that this is a natural way for the young toddler to learn about differences, particularly when the parent is ready to respond to the questions which are bound to come up. I would object to this only if the children became too stimulated by mutual looking and if they got out of hand with silliness and fighting—two very common ways of showing sexual excitement. If overstimulation occurs, I'd toilet them separately and tell them why. I would say I noticed that toileting them together makes them too excited. I'd ask them what they wanted to know. Here again it is "no" to the activity and "yes" to the discussion. Overexcitement may occur among members of the same sex too, in which case the same recommendation prevails.

Small issues that need a special approach include motels, campers, and overnight guests. Try to separate the sexes in different rooms if you can. If you are stuck and find you are all piled into one room, have a single bed, cot, or sleeping bag for each person. Dress for bed in the bathroom. Postpone your own sexual activity until complete privacy is assured. This will keep things as neutral as possible.

INVASIONS OF PRIVACY

Some places, like your local swimming pool or your neighborhood community center, may not offer dressing privacy. Your children may be exposed to the nudity of other families. This is hardest on the under-five group. Again, if this should happen, discuss it. If the child wants to know about sex differences, explain. Seeing a stranger undressed does not generally cause him as much worry as seeing a member of his immediate family unclothed. The stranger is not important to the child, and therefore the sight of him or her naked is less charged with feelings.

Obviously there will be casual invasions of privacy, even at home. People may walk in on each other by mistake. Don't overreact or convey horror to the child. Minor infractions of the general rule do not necessarily make for future psychological problems. Yet I firmly believe that promoting respect for privacy and modesty is better for your children.

One father disagreed with me. "My daughter is doing beautifully at Radcliffe and she was raised without this nonsense," he sputtered.

Children do vary in their ability to withstand excitement. Also, when sensible discipline prevails in other areas of a child's life, this limit setting may help the child deal with the questions raised by sexual differences in a positive way. But it is hard to know from outside observation just what is going on inside a particular individual. As this father's angry reaction demonstrates, neither he nor, for that matter, any of us is happy about past mistakes. We tend, in the most human way, to defend what is already done.

PREVENTIVE MEDICINE

I suggest to those of you just starting out that modesty is good preventive medicine. By school age your child will probably know about sex differences and how babies are born —at least he will know the baby has grown in the mother's body. For those of you who have not yet given information to school-age children, make the effort now. It's best when it comes from you. Observations of a pregnant woman give you an opportunity to lead into the subject; seeing a friend's baby diapered may provide a chance for discussion. By the age of seven or eight, your child is ready for a visit to the local health museum, if your city has one. (Before this time the size and nature of the exhibits can be overwhelming.) At eight years of age he can read one of the suggested books for himself. For the nonquestioning child, leaving the books around gives tacit permission to his curiosity. Acknowledge with him that he's interested. Show acceptance of his curiosity. This tone is appropriate at any age.

Later on, when your children are grown, they may accuse you of never having told them the facts. It's a strange business, this forgetting. But you will have helped them despite their faulty memory because in the part of the childish mind where demons once played, you introduced reason and clarity. Their emotional responses to their more mature and urgent impulses benefit from that very real, if unconsciously forgotten, knowledge.

VII
Use of the Parallel Story

"There once was a little boy. His name was Billy." Danny, age three, gets closer to mother on the couch. "There was a Mommy and a Daddy living with him but he was the *only child*," she goes on. Danny nods contentedly. This is the "Billy story" he has asked his mother to tell him every night for the past two weeks. He knows what she is going to say before she says it but he wants to hear what is coming anyhow.

"Billy's Mommy used to take him to the store," says Dan's mother. "They bought things to eat and Billy liked to have his mother make him lunch." She enlarges on the story and inserts elements of her own child's life into it. "His favorite was peanut butter and jelly." She stresses how much Billy liked being the *only one*. Dan is rapt with attention.

"And then I went to the zoo with Daddy," he adds. "Don't forget the monkeys." He likes the parallel she draws because it gives him a chance to ruminate about his life experiences. When we consider how much of growing up is an assault on the egocentric position of babyhood, we can understand his enjoyment of the story better.

"And then came a baby brother," his mother goes on.

"Billy didn't like that one bit," Danny nods in response to

this. "The baby can't even throw a ball!"

His mother agrees. "Billy wanted a friend to play with, and instead he got a baby!"

"Babies stink!" Dan's voice rises. "They make poop in their pants!" His pride in his own rather recent accomplishment is evidenced in his disdain.

"The hardest part for Billy was that he wasn't the only child any more. He liked being the only one. Before the baby came he used to have his Mommy all to himself."

"And you walk him while I'm at school!" The enormity of her offense overwhelms Dan for a moment.

"Billy hated to be away. He thought his mother and the baby were having too much fun."

WHY STORIES ARE VALUABLE

You get the idea. By telling a story you recognize with your child that emotions exist; you dignify them and admit your child's right to them. In this way you make his feelings more explicable to him.

In our parental role as educators we have little difficulty in telling a child about the real world. "This is your nose." "Here is your cup." We teach words for things. It is an objective process, and we move on easily to the properties of things.

"The stove is hot."

We take the next step and draw a conclusion for him.

"You mustn't touch."

We stand between the property of hot and the consequence of injury. This is so self-evident it hardly bears examination.

But we often have great difficulty talking directly to the child about his emotional life. That is why the parallel story is so valuable. It is an education that teaches him about his inner world. He learns about feelings. These feelings may have small relationship to the real world. Was Billy ever *really* the only one? Wasn't there a father and didn't his mother have interests of her own which had value for her despite his childish wishes to the contrary?

A few years ago a Broadway play, *Rosencrantz & Guildenstern Are Dead,* demonstrated how Hamlet's worries appeared to the nonprincipals. Snatches of conversation were overhead by the servingmen; the major dramas of the important characters were distorted, since only parts of them were perceived. This is how life is for the child. His inability to understand the total picture is a feature of childhood. In all of these chapters the message is the same. You are filling in the gaps which he can't understand. With your better understanding of where he is in the process of development, you try to give him information that he can absorb. Knowing the normal distresses that most children are subject to in the course of growing up can give you clues. These provide the content of the stories you can make up to enlarge his perceiving abilities.

SIBLING RIVALRY

Parallel stories can go in any direction. The young child's envy of an older sibling's skills can be dealt with in another story.

"Once there was a little boy named Johnny. He was three years old. He had a big sister, Ann, who was five. Ann went to school every day. Johnny liked to do everything Ann could do."

You take it from there and improvise with particular elements that are meaningful for him. "Ann could ride a bike and count numbers." You might pause here to see if he wants to tell you something. Sometimes he gets into the story, as Danny did. Sometimes he sits there blankly, and sometimes he runs around acting like he isn't listening at all. Don't be discouraged. Often he never replies. This does not mean that he isn't listening. To your astonishment, he may ask for the story months later, or he may refer to it casually in another connection. But it is true that you may never get a concrete response. Nevertheless, go on.

"Johnny wished he could ride a bike. He wished he could do these grownup things." It is not difficult to see that you are on target because Johnny has shown in so many ways that his jealousy makes life difficult for him. "It was hard for Johnny to wait until he was able to do the things that Ann could do." You may wish to rush to the happy ending. "But every day Johnny was growing older. One day he was able to ride a bike. One day he could go to school and learn to read."

There is nothing wrong with a happy ending such as this. In fact, most children's stories conclude on such a note, with problems finally getting settled in a comforting way. But the strength of your made-to-fit stories is that you need not rush to make things okay too fast. Negative feelings, which most of us were not allowed to express in our own childhood, take time to unroll. In general, because of our own rearing, we don't like to hear about them either. Everyone wants things to be harmonious and serene—particularly grandparents and well-meaning friends who prefer the untroubled surface of things. What they don't understand is that negative feelings exist everywhere, whether the feelings are acknowledged or not. If you understand that your child's acceptance of his own bad feelings will ultimately help him to cope better and enable him to love his siblings better (eventually, that is), you may find the strength to allow him to express difficult emotions. After all, it is the bad feelings that cause all the trouble. The good feelings take care of themselves.

THE NEW ARRIVAL

The story can be used as early as two years of age. Usually before that time you do better in being direct and and talking to your child in terms of what is happening to him now. If you come home with a new baby when your child is twenty-two months old, don't think he doesn't have strong feelings just because he doesn't have the words. Voice his feelings for him. "Sometimes when you see Mommy feed the baby, you wish you could be a baby." One mother served juice and crackers to her toddler when she breast-fed the newborn. In this way she was giving the older child as well as the infant a feeding which he loved, but she did so in a manner that was appropriate to his age.

In addition to actively responding to your child's need, you can use words to explain the act. Tell him why you are doing something. "You can have a snack too. This is a hard time for you. You used to be the only one." This helps give even the very young toddler an understanding of what is happening. Perhaps it leaves memory traces in his head. These can be called upon at a later time when feelings bedevil him and he needs to sort them out for himself. In short, it promotes the development of insight.

THE MIDDLE CHILD

The middle child needs his own story. (He is in the middle whether he's smack in the middle, or second, third, fourth, or more.) The story can touch upon elements that are familiar to him. "There once was a little girl named Polly. She had an older brother and a very big sister. Her big brother played baseball a lot. Her sister was like Mommy. She took care of Polly sometimes, and she was even bossy." You can warm to the custom-made story with, "Polly did not like her big sister telling her what to do. She wanted to take care of the new baby herself."

Polly agrees vigorously. She has been a pretty bossy sister herself to the six-month-old newcomer, Larry.

"It was hard to be in the middle. The big kids stayed up later and even babysat, and Larry was so cute, everyone paid so much attention to him." You can stay with the theme that those ahead of the middle child can do more things and have more privileges. You also express the pull of wanting to be a baby, since gratifications abound for the little one, and everyone responds to a baby. You can use the phrase "left-out feelings" to describe the state of the child in the story. Labeling feelings is the first step in their mastery.

Sometimes a child will recognize that you are talking directly to him. You can acknowledge his recognition. He may prefer direct discussion, and it is easy enough to drop the story in that case. The main reason for employing the story is the greater neutrality it brings to highly charged topics. If he prefers to drop the pretense, do so.

You don't have to have an ending to these stories. Generally young children are so intent on hearing their feelings voiced they don't even notice the limitations of the plot. If you've acknowledged that it's a made-up story you can say, "We'll make up some more tomorrow." Maybe he'll give you ideas about how to proceed. If you've told the story as a genuine happening, stay with that. In all of these methods you are telling the child about himself and showing him respect for his many parts, the bad as well as the good. You help him like himself more as he accepts what he feels, *no matter in what direction it takes him.*

THOUGHTS ARE NOT ACTIONS

There is where we differ from parents of an earlier age. The Victorians expected good behavior from their children. The "no-nos" were clear and the discipline (most often punishment) was exacting. That system led to difficulty because the feelings which precipitated the action were denied as well.

Children were told how they felt. And they were told they felt positively.

"We love one another."

"You love babies, don't you?"

For a child who felt otherwise, an inner split often occurred. He was cut off from part of himself. He by no means felt loving at all times, so self-criticism and self-loathing followed. He hated himself for his angry thoughts.

But thoughts are not actions, and this is an important distinction. It is important to get over our prejudice about them. Thoughts are of all kinds, hateful and nasty as well as loving and kind.

Acknowledging that thoughts exist is only the truth. The child is stronger for it and better integrated as a human being. As adults we don't remember all our negative childhood feelings because we have forgotten the earliest years; but if we know something of our own conflicting feelings, how much richer and wiser we are! Self-knowledge, even of the simple variety I am talking about here (such as jealousy of a sibling or the wish to be first), enables us to get a handle on ourselves, and we are able to behave better.

The story provides an outlet for the unacceptable side of human nature without allowing these feelings to be put into unacceptable action. It is a safe release for the child, as his feelings are accepted in a removed way. The story is about *his* feelings, but it is not only about him. Billy has the same feelings Danny does. Through a story a child learns that his feelings are okay, that indeed others have sad and angry feelings too. You need not scold a child for having bad thoughts, as parents did in an earlier time. Today we have a more balanced view of human nature which recognizes that wretched thoughts exist and that people are not evil for having them. Acting on them is another matter, however. You repeat, "You can feel and say it, but you can't do it."

ACKNOWLEDGING THE GOOD AND THE BAD

Are you being a hypocrite to acknowledge to each child that he has a unique position and a unique response to that position? No. Each child does have a special place. All you are doing is bearing witness to the right of the child to have his feelings (random, inconsistent, hostile, selfish, or whatever) accepted. These feelings change rapidly in the course of growing up. The child who hates a sibling today may love him tomorrow. The chances are better that this will happen if the nasty side is not denied.

But don't retreat from your own judgment of what you expect in behavior. "Even though you are mad at Billy, you can't hurt him" has to be the repeated refrain. A reason is not the same as an excuse. For the younger child of two or two and a half who needs physical release, a substitute punching bag can be provided. Words are not yet readily available to him. For the three-to-five-year-old, however, words are more useful, and the story is a way of using words which apply directly to him.

The Victorian stance about feelings often led to hypocrisy because it denied the existence of negative feelings. If feelings were recognized, a moral judgment was passed on the sinner. Thoughts were confused with actions, and people were made to feel guilty for things they had never done. Wise children learned soon enough to simulate socially acceptable feelings, although this was not the same as actually feeling them.

Now you can have it both ways. You can help civilize your child in terms of graded expectation (much as the Victorians did), but you can also help the process along by an honest admission of the intermittently villainous feelings that beset everyone. You too pass a moral judgment. "Cruelty is bad," you say. But you make the distinction between feeling something and doing it. You acknowledge that the child may have a conflict but you expect him to do better. He learns to prefer the civilized way as you are consistent in expecting it of him. The parallel story, in effect, helps admit the inadmissible but does not permit the unpermissible.

He says, "I want it."

You say, "No."

He says, "It's mine."

You say, "Share."

The disagreement in these exchanges is unavoidable.

There is a necessary conflict between infantile behavior and adult socialization. When you tell a story you soften the confrontation by your understanding. You say, "Ellen didn't want to share. She wanted to have the cake all to herself. It was hard to give her friend a piece." Ellen may agree with you on this. "But she did it," you add. "It's not easy, but friends learn to share. Someday Karen will give you a piece of cake when you want it."

Generalizing can be useful in a story. "Other little boys and girls often feel this way." A child's self-esteem takes less of a beating when he learns that others share his plight.

A VIEW OF THE TABLE

The story can be used in any number of life situations that cause distress for children, including those that have been discussed in the book as well as any unique ones of your own. The parallel story allows the child to be the judge and to see all sides of an issue. It gives him a view of the table, which in his infancy he couldn't reach. Sometimes he takes pleasure in the cruelty of a familiar fairytale in a book. Sometimes he enjoys the supermorality of a story in which only goodness and kindness prevail. Learning that many feelings are allowable (if deeds are not) increases maturity and self-control. The knowledge that you can feel two ways about someone —love and hate are often close—and that the world doesn't come to an end is a genuine comfort to a child.

You may be surprised at the depth of feeling your child reveals in response to the story. It tells him how much you understand him and how fully you accept him. But don't expect to be appreciated every time you tell the story. Sometimes it gets too close to the bone, and the child tunes out. He doesn't want to understand what you are saying. That's the time to stop. Don't ruin the effectiveness of the parallel story by overdoing it.

VIII
Temporary Separations

"When you go away, Mommy, it's cold," says three-year-old Ruth Ann. "Don't go," she adds.

Not all children are able to express themselves so graphically, yet all children react to separation from loved ones, and the younger they are, the more anguish they feel. These are not separation problems. These are separation feelings, and they are perfectly normal. They never disappear entirely. Even adults show traces of them. Have you ever noticed your own letdown feeling when someone you care about takes a plane? Or the emptiness of the house when your husband is on a trip? It is painful to be separated from someone you love, and for the child under three it is practically unbearable. His relationship to you is his lifeline.

Your child develops physically and emotionally as a result of the bond you build by caring for him. It takes him months, in the beginning, to know you are you. At about seven or eight months old he shows very clearly that it is only you that he wants. When he develops locomotion, in the second year, he loves to get away from you—but not for long. And he doesn't like it one bit when you go away from him. This is one of the reasons that he keeps returning to check you out. He likes having Mommy near, even though he enjoys his independence and runs away from her at every chance. But don't confuse growing independence with lessening need.

Between eight and eighteen months he is particularly susceptible to your leaving him. "He won't let me out of his sight" is a frequent complaint. It is important to realize that these reactions are typical and that they occur less often as his ability to judge time improves. In the preverbal stage the child finds certain things more difficult, and separation is one of them. When he is able to voice his concern, as he starts to talk, and understand your words of reassurance, he learns that he needn't fear what is the basic concern of his young life—abandonment.

KEEP EARLY SEPARATIONS BRIEF

Because you are so central to the child's development before the age of two, it is best to keep early separations brief. Certainly between eight and eighteen months he has more difficulty accepting your absence than at a later date. An afternoon or an evening away is as much as he can tolerate, given the limitations of his small intellect and his all-important need for your presence. If you have left him for a longer interval and have had no problems with him as a result, it may be that he is one of those children with a greater ability to cope with strain. But you should recognize that leaving you does put pressure on him. The "go away but come back" concept isn't firm in his mind until toward the end of his second year. Your comings and goings teach him about it gradually. He may react strongly to even short separations. Such reactions are normal and to be expected because his concept of time is so poorly developed. Making friends with other mothers in similar circumstances can help you ease the bind of a child-centered world at this time.

Between the ages of two and three he can cope somewhat better, but he still does not respond well to your being away for more than two or three days at a time. Some mothers have assumed that by being away a lot they are training the child to accept their absence and helping to build his independence. But such an approach asks more of the very young child than he can handle. The steps to independence are gradual ones. You increase your expectations as he grows older.

Keeping separations short before age three may not always be possible. Perhaps you are having another baby, or must have an operation, or need to help your sister's family in a time of crisis. Vacations away from children are also imperative, and I would have tunnel vision indeed if I did not recognize that other factors play a part in a busy mother's life. For the time being, however, let's stay with the ideal (never realized by anyone, please understand) and recognize that if you must leave a young child, he will find it difficult to accept your absence.

IF YOU MUST GET AWAY

If you need to get off with your husband for a child-free vacation (who doesn't need this at times?), it is better to take a number of short trips than to be away *once* for a long interval. A series of weekend overnights can relieve the tension for you and educate the very young to the reality of your return. Sometimes they are so dreadful when you return that you wonder if it was worth it. It is. For you it is a break-in routine; for them it is a maturing experience.

One mother announced as she was leaving my office that she was going on a trip in two days. "How shall I prepare my two-year-old?" she asked.

"Will you kill him if you don't go?" I asked.

"No question about it," she answered.

Not one to encourage infanticide, I helped her plan things in the time she had. All of us have to work within the limits of the possible. But knowing the ideal can help us plan when we have some control over choices. Between one and a half and two and a half the child may give you a hard time when you go, but he is better able to tolerate your going than the younger child.

If you must leave, speak to your child beforehand. If he's still in the preverbal stage, talk anyway. Talk as if he's five years old. His understanding outstrips his ability to talk. Leave something of yours with him when you go—an old sweater, a scarf, any belonging. This serves as a stand-in for your presence. For the older child, pictures are useful. Having the babysitter talk about you while you are away is also fine.

One sitter drew a map of the place mother and father were going. She had blown up eight balloons for the eight days they would be away. Each day she had Margaret and Teddy break one balloon, and this seemed to help them understand the time concept. Crossing days off on a calendar is another way of helping children recognize that time does move.

THE FIRST VACATION

After the age of three a child can tolerate a separation of a week more easily. You can now plan a vacation and talk about it ahead of time with your child. Parents often hate to do this because it is like asking for a thunderstorm. The child becomes angry or tearful or pleading—"Why can't I go?"—and the joy of getting away diminishes with each scene. What you'd like to do is sneak away or tell him at bedtime that you are leaving the very next morning. This same desire for peace at any price lies behind telling the child who is going in for a tonsillectomy that he is going to a "nice place where you will eat ice cream." You want to escape his wrath and sorrow.

This is one time when genuine courage on your part is required. The sooner you tell him the facts and allow him to feel his distress, the better he will be able to manage while you are gone. In this sense, bad is good. In the long run you will find that his independence has been strengthened by your effort to help him meet a difficult event. By giving him a chance to anticipate the separation, you allow him to deal with the fact of your leaving, the feelings that come as he anticipates it, and finally the fact that you will be coming back. That he is upset before you leave in no way means he will not be able to cope; in fact, the opposite is true. When you let him air the sad, angry, or fearful feelings while you are there, he has the comfort of your understanding and explaining. This stands him in good stead when you are not there. "Mommy come back. It's okay," said two-year-old Roger as he patted his own hand.

This bubbling up of feeling at a time of separation is all to the good, although it can be very hard for a parent to take. Your goal, in helping him face a painful situation such as a good-by from a loved one, is to allow his distressed feelings expression.

Children under five are given to emotion of great depth, and while it is true that parental expectation leads to good behavior, it is also true that allowing painful feelings to be expressed makes for a more genuine accommodation in time. It is better for him that you hear his crying and witness his bad tempers. It is not pleasant, but it builds toward a later serenity. It also builds a trust in you. Over the years he knows you are to be counted on to understand him.

MASTERING SEPARATION

An increase in your expectation that he can manage apart from you for longer intervals recognizes the contribution of maturation. That is to say, as he gets older he can tolerate your absence better. As he understands more and is able to do some things for himself, he is better able to cope with your demands. He doesn't feel so helpless in the face of what he regards as your desertion.

One two-and-a-half-year-old became very balky when his

mother left him for a series of afternoon appointments. She took up with him the fact that he was angry. (He'd had a tantrum and smashed a toy.) It was hard to be left behind. The next time she left him he announced, "And now *I* go by-by!" He had seized his coat and was halfway out the door before she could stop him. He glared at her for the interference. "I go," he said emphatically. "You stay. I go by-by. You stay home." A moment later he returned and patted her hand. "Mommy feel bad. Okay, Mommy." He had turned the tables on her neatly and was doing to her *actively* what he had experienced passively.

This is quite an advance in emotional mastery. It lies behind many pediatricians' recommendations that young children be encouraged to give their dolls shots after a doctor's visit. It turns the situation around and lets the children be the active inflicters of pain rather than the helpless receivers. It defuses a lot of anger that normally is aroused when a person is helpless in the face of pain—and separation is pain.

Mastery of separation is better handled on a piecemeal basis. Each time you leave he learns more about the world of reality. Once again you tell him the facts. "I have to leave." Don't deny it or sneak out to avoid a stormy scene. Prepare him early enough so he can deal with the feeling *before* you go. When you finally have to go—go! If you have fudged it in the past, admit now that that was a mistake and tell him you think it important that he know what is what.

BABYSITTERS

Certainly mothers need time away from their children if they are to keep their sanity. The importance of having a reliable sitter (whether a neighbor, a schoolgirl, or a relative) cannot be overstressed. It helps the child tremendously if the same person is there each time you go away. The child then begins to relate to that person, and the constancy of the same person helps him adapt more successfully. It may not be easy to find a steady sitter in our mobile age. But it can be done if you recognize its importance. Look for someone who is friendly, competent, and *there*. If you need to use a sitter he doesn't know, have her visit your home beforehand to get acquainted. A babysitting session is practice for him. Again I am speaking of the ideal. When circumstances are less than ideal, be prepared to pay the price. In clinging. In talking. In working him back to his former security. Keeping children together rather than farming them out individually is very helpful. Older siblings help little ones a great deal.

Pools of young mothers for children under three, though handy and inexpensive, often make things harder for toddlers. The kids have to relate to too many people, and often normal separation feelings get lost in the shuffle. If you are in a pool, try to limit the reciprocal sitting to *one* friend. There's less stress for him in that.

NURSERY SCHOOLS

If you enroll your three-year-old in a nursery school, or its improvised equivalent, you should arrange to stay with him at school for several days. Three days is adequate; a week is better. Sometimes several weeks are required and occasionally even more time is necessary. If your school discourages parental involvement (even good ones have been known to send a bus), try to persuade the teachers to let the separation process happen. You can ask to sit in an outer office. Your child can be given permission to run out to see you at times when he needs to check. Talk with him at home each day about the fact that you are reducing the time you spend at school the next day. This gives him a chance to cope with his feelings. At three it's better if you can take your child to school in the beginning. Carpools and buses are more acceptable to him at four. Here again it is a gradual process.

A child feels three sorts of emotions during a separation

from parents—sadness, anger, and fear. You may see all, one, or none of these as he struggles to adapt to new conditions. Often it may not be clear that he is reacting to a separation at all. He may act as if he is angry at something else or sad about an entirely different issue. Or he may show no overt response, as was true with four-year-old Kathleen.

On Kathy's first day at school she haunted the front window of the nursery, searching for her mother. At the close of school, when she saw her mother walking up the path, she turned her back on her and nonchalantly began to paint. Her mother's face, bright with expectation when she arrived, fell. "She's so indifferent," she said to the teacher. "She didn't miss me at all."

PARTING IS NOT SWEET SORROW

Regardless of what you see, sadness and anger about separation are normal. Parting is not such sweet sorrow for the very young child. You've caused him pain so he is resentful. Fear may not be present, but if it is, it may be disguised. You may see a stirring up of fears at night (remember, bedtime is separation too) as a reaction to his separation from you during the day. If he wants bad things to happen to you because you left him (tit for tat is characteristic of the thinking of children under five), he may then be afraid that they will. His love for you activates concern for your welfare, and often a temporary clinging is noticeable at separation time. By handling separations in a slow and gradual fashion, you will find that these feelings lessen. Once again, talk is the most helpful way to make this happen.

Four-year-old Nancy was told she had to go to nursery school because her parents thought it was good for her. This was a sensible decision on their part. What made Nancy more agreeable to the plan was their talking to her about her feelings of strangeness at school. They had moved from another city six months before. Now they talked about her old friends and how much she missed them. She was lively at this point and warmed to the subject. She missed her friends. She hated the new town. Why had they moved? She cried about the old house; she liked her wallpaper in that house better. Her parents acknowledged how hard all this was. They said it would take time to get used to the new school. But then when they insisted she comply, she went easily and the adaptation process was under way.

Once more, the point is that there are *always* feelings about separation. When we don't see or hear about them it is because we haven't given them a chance to surface. Children clue in very fast to what's tolerable for us and what isn't. If you can talk to them honestly ahead of time, allow them to express their feelings in words, and then leave as planned (I recognize that the problem may then be to enjoy yourself), you will have given them a chance to master the most basic infantile anxiety.

In a way, dealing with the separation feelings of little ones is like writing a term paper. In preparing a term paper, you first state what you are going to do. Then you do it. Then you describe what you did. Introduction. Body. Conclusion. There is a similar approach to dealing with separation:

1. You tell your child what is going to happen.
2. It happens.
3. You talk to him about what happened.

SUDDEN SEPARATIONS

There are times when emergencies make it impossible to follow these recommendations. Nevertheless, there are still things that can be done. If you go into labor in the middle of the night, wake your toddler and tell him you're going. Call him on the telephone the next day. Send a toy or hospital trinket via Daddy. Supply the sitter with some small toys (one for each day) to give him from you. This much can be planned in advance. Keep communication open. He may retaliate and ignore you when you return. If so, talk about that. Talk about his disappointment, his missing you. You may need to provide the words for him, but you can be sure he will be listening intently and be relieved at being understood.

If an even greater emergency arises and you are unable to prepare your child, have someone else do it. Fathers—or sensitive neighbors or friends—come in handy at times like these. They can help the child talk over his feelings about your sudden departure.

He may cling for a while after a surprise separation. You may find this very annoying, particularly if he is four or five and seemed beyond the clinging stage when you left. But he needs to do this for a while. Here again talk is helpful. He might need a night light, just as if he were a baby again. That is okay, but *don't* lie in bed with him or be a prisoner to his every whim. Try not to let guilt make you a victim of infantile tyranny. *Do* recognize fear when you see it and slowly wean him back to his former level of maturity. You may need to sit near the door of his room at night if irrational fears spring up. Recognize, however, that they are temporary and reduce the time you give to this each day. It is a way of unrolling worry backward.

It is useful to hold up the goal of managing by encouraging his feelings *first*. "You used to be okay about Mommy's going." He still clings to your skirts. "But then I went away for a long time." (Three days to the toddler feels like three years.) He holds tighter. "Now you're afraid I won't come back." He nods vigorously. "But I will." If an impasse such as this has developed, make your first absence after the separation brief—say, a half hour. The second absence, an hour. Work up to an afternoon. His irrational anxiety will diminish with each return.

Concise language is useful.

"Mommy goes away."

"Mommy comes back."

For the preverbal child, it helps to keep him in his own home when you leave because it is familiar and therefore feels safe. It is better to have grandmother come stay at your house than to drop him at hers, unless, of course, he is there frequently and knows it well. Children feel separation from their homes very acutely.

On one family vacation the parents took everyone along. Alec, who was two, complained constantly. "I miss my upstairs and my downstairs," he said. Here he was missing *place*, not people. But these complaints, though valid for him at this age, were trivial. Everyone had a good time, including Alec.

Children of three and four take all of this better. Their time concepts are clearer and they can do many things themselves.

MOVING

House moving may prove to be a genuine hardship for children of any age. Here again, talking about it ahead of time and allowing normal negative feelings to be expressed make the final moving day easier. Some parents take pictures of the old house before they leave. Describing the new house can also be useful. One mother bought play furniture and a toy van to help relieve her three-year-old's anxiety about the move. Any realistic preparation you do pays off by strengthening your child's ability to cope. Rehearsal is the name of the game. Here again, you are assisting the child's maturing. Don't be surprised, however, to find that more talk will be required after the move, no matter how well you have prepared for it. The child will complain about changes anyway —simply because he likes things which are familiar. Time is on your side as he slowly makes new friends and begins to be part of the new community.

Talking about painful feelings with children, particularly when you cannot alter a fact, is not easy. Most of us were raised with such time-honored adages as "Let sleeping dogs lie" and "Don't cry over spilled milk." The idea that ventilating feelings can help the coping process is a new one for most of us. Yet, if we stop to think of situations in our own lives where we were allowed to express our feelings in an honest way, we will gain some appreciation of what a relief such candor offers to the young child.

THE WORKING MOTHER

Implicit in all this is the assumption that you will be staying home with your child and taking care of him, at least for the preschool years. With all the current interest in careers for women, this may not be the course you will choose. No one can decide this for you, and you will need to weigh the various factors for yourself. Economic needs can play a part in such a decision, but emotional factors (a mother's need to work for her own satisfaction, for example) are equally important as you chart your course.

The child's needs, however, cannot be disregarded. His development rests on establishing a strong attachment to one person who will be a constant presence for him. The complexities and resolutions of the various phases of development do not proceed normally if a child is not given the opportunity of relating to one central person. If it appears that you must work or be away from home a great deal, it is important that you delegate the mothering functions to a person who will really take them over. Good physical care by a series of babysitters is not enough. A substitute mother is required, and the person who performs this function needs your guidance in fulfilling the various responsibilities that good mothering entails. The concept of mother as educator requires that you teach your substitute how to be the educator. And the guiding principle of this chapter—that the smaller the child, the smaller the separation interval—needs to be thoroughly understood by the mother substitute.

For those of you who want to combine a career and motherhood, you can take heart. Women are living longer than ever before, and it is an investment in the future to stay home with little ones until school starts (or at least until nursery school starts at age three) so that they can get the emotional base they need for healthy development. When you do go back to pick up your career, you can enjoy your work and know that your children have been given the start they need. If you delay going to work until they are six or older, they can handle your departure better. What is more important, you also can handle it better. Older children can afford to be proud of a working mother and may even become more independent because they have had to pitch in. Timing is of the essence here.

For those of you who have no choice but to work, there are still many constructive things you can do to provide the kind of mothering care that enhances development. Try to avoid day-care centers for the child under three, as they don't offer the individual attention the very young child needs. Instead, try to select a motherly-type person to stand in for you. (If necessity later requires a change of sitters, talk to the child about his separation feelings from her and visit her if possible. In this way he is helped to make the transition to the new sitter.) Spend time with him evenings and weekends. Talk with him about his feelings and allow him to voice his concerns. Take him to see your office or plant so he can visualize you in a setting. Talk about what you do. Arrange matters so that he can call you if he needs to. These are not small things and they can make a great deal of difference to your child. Your relationship will grow as you exert the daily effort. Naturally, his love for his mother substitute may bring you a pang at times, but his attachment to her is good for his growing up. When he is older, it will enable him to love you better. (Loving takes practice.)

And don't forget yourself as well. You need to make time for some adult satisfactions too, or child rearing can become onerous and guilt-ridden. Children sense guilt feelings and often try to take advantage of them. The working mother has no reason not to impose the same discipline and have the same expectations for her children as any other mother.

You may be tempted to overindulge your children because you are away from them so much. Resist that temptation. Children grow better in a structured environment. You can give your children a solid beginning even if circumstances don't permit you to be with them full time.

Either way, the early years pass soon enough. And it's no small satisfaction to know that you were instrumental in rearing a well-adjusted human being from the sprawling bundle of life with which you began.

IX
Large Separations: Death

Most separations are controllable. You have the final say on when you will be leaving, when you will be coming back, and where your children will be staying while you are gone. Even small separations require special handling, but generally they are manageable once you accept that fact that your absence is significant to your child.

There are separations, however, which are not controllable, and both you and your child must struggle with the helpless feelings they evoke. Death is the most difficult of all these. It is final, and it is a permanent loss. There are no concrete, satisfying answers to why a person dies. The way we respond depends on our own life history. We may respond in ways we could not have predicted, for every time death strikes someone close to us, it is new—even if we have dealt with death many times in the past. Death is always new. The person lost has never gone forever before.

Here is a place where our intellect tries to serve us. We know and have known for many years that all living things die. Man is part of this cycle. We acknowledge the inevitability of death when we attend a funeral, pay a tribute to a friend, visit a widow. But even as we do this, we want to rush past. We mourn our own loss in the person gone, and often we find his family's grief too painful to witness. These times remind us most poignantly of our own mortality.

What is strange is that each time a loved one dies, it comes as a shock; death seems an invader. It is as if our intellect knows something that our feelings reject. Almost all of us live as if death will not happen to us or our loved ones, as if death is something that happens to other people. Although we know the facts with our minds, we reject them with our hearts. In that way, we are able to function well on a daily basis and live as if there were no end to the tomorrows.

When loss comes, adults lose the sense of control that sustains them in their daily lives; they feel helpless. It is therefore much harder to deal with your children's loss when you are trying to cope with your own.

It might not be possible. If the person who died was very close to you, you may not be able to help your children very much at all. Facing your own feelings may be all that you have the emotional energy for. You will be embarked on a long process of feeling your sorrow over and over. The feelings death brings are complex and varied. You may feel sorrow at one time, remorse at another. You may be irrationally angry at the person who died. (It was his leaving which caused you the pain, wasn't it?) You can feel relief that the person's anguish may be over. Guilt may follow, or depression—a feeling that life isn't worth living without the other person. Sometimes a forced gaiety ensues.

So you are busy emotionally, not just for the week or two when people pay calls but for months and possibly for years.

In the real world of action, however, what you do is *do and make do.* You struggle to adapt, and what aids you most at this difficult time is your fundamental resilience.

"WHO WILL TAKE CARE OF ME?"

Where children differ from adults in this regard is in their immaturity. They too have profound feelings of loss; they too share in the bewilderment that confronts all of us at a time when no earthly claim can make a difference. But they are children. And what characterizes the child (particularly the very young child) is his absorption in himself. What matters most for him is how the loss relates to him and to his needs. If the person who died was his caretaker (mother or substitute mother), his first need is to be assured that someone will take care of him. Often he will not be able to express his sorrow until he has a relationship with the new person. He has to have continuity before the trauma can be dealt with.

"Who will take care of me?" asked four-year-old Kevin when his mother died. When an aunt stepped in and assumed his daily care, then and only then could he miss his mother. A child of five, when told of her mother's death, attached herself to the minister's wife and could make no reference to her loss until she established a permanent relationship with a cousin who came forward. She had to reestablish the life-lines before she could let herself feel. Sometimes we mistake children's lack of demonstrable sorrow as an absence of feeling. We think they are callous or too young to realize the finality of death.

As adults we are reluctant to see children suffer pain. We often try to put a good face on things. "Grandpa is up in heaven. He is happy there." We want to soften the blow because we recognize their immaturity and comprehend that their understanding is limited.

Yet the explanations we give can never be really adequate, because no one knows for sure when abstract thought takes place in a child's mind. The child tends to think concretely. When we tell him about heaven he wants to know where it is; he knows what he can see, and if it's up in the sky, how did Grandpa get there? Still, if your religion includes belief in an afterlife and you can talk of it with conviction, it may help soothe the desperate, once-and-for-all feeling death brings to everyone. If you do not believe in an afterlife, acknowledging you don't know everything may allow the child to invent stories that serve him temporarily. Telling the truth as you see it is best.

Certainly how the child views death depends on many factors—his age, who the lost person was, whether the person suffered sudden or lingering death, whether or not the child witnessed the dying. All these affect him in different ways, and over a period of time his views of the event will change and change again. As his intelligence grows, he can take in the facts better. As with everything else, the questions he asks can be dealt with over and over.

STATING THE FACTS

Just what are these facts that need statement? The facts are what we on earth know with our senses. For the child under four, the major points are that the person died and can't come back.

"He wants to," said the mother of a three-year-old who lost his father. "He wants to but he can't." The child's feelings of loss surfaced as others "came back" but not his father. Slowly and over a period of time other realistic elements may be added.

"His body is in a box. No, he isn't sleeping. No, he doesn't get hungry or need clothes. No, he has no pain. He is in the ground. Yes, we miss him very much."

In your own words you state the following facts as the child asks about them. You don't give it to him all at once:

1. The person died.
2. He stopped living and breathing. He can't feel.
3. He is buried in the ground. Nothing can hurt him.
4. He isn't coming back.
5. We are sad because we miss him.

This last point is made with each of the others. Separation is the essential message for the younger child. He learns, as we all do, by the absence of the person.

Grief is of course a private matter, and the public demon-stration of it may tell little of one's relationship to the person gone. But it is helpful not to hide your sadness from your children. A stiff upper lip may be admirable for your life in the outside world, but sorrow is real. Certainly in the privacy of your home, it should be expressed. Tears may not be your style, but if they are, let them fall. Tell the child why you are crying. It shows him that being in touch with feelings is human and not shameful. Sorrow should not be simply toler-ated; it should be seen as something of value. If tight-lipped silence is your style, let him know verbally that you are sad. Tell him it takes time to get over feeling awful.

"No, I am not angry."

"Yes, I still love you even though I look upset. It is just that I am missing Uncle Bill."

Sometimes children find it hard to accept your sorrow. "Stop crying!" ordered Peter. He didn't want to be upset. Later he brought his mother a tissue. "That's for when you feel sad about Daddy."

One little girl whose brother was killed in a car crash told me she wished she was the one who had died. I asked why.

"They don't talk to me," she said of her parents. "My mother just sits and looks out the window. They don't care about me! All they care about is him!"

Her parents had no idea that she felt this way. Their own loss was so overwhelming that they were barely in touch with her. Talk would have helped in this case. Even though noth-ing can be changed realistically by talking, there is relief in knowing that it is okay to feel. Sometimes feelings of sorrow need to be voiced many times. The more sensitive members of the clergy are aware of this when they visit a bereaved family, not only formally one or two times after the loss, but informally many months later. Grief is felt for a long time.

When you cannot manage to talk to the children because of your own misery, ask family members or close friends to do it for you. They are not as emotionally involved as you are; they can tell the children the facts and can help them during the crisis. They can be available for answering any questions the children may have. Delegating the talking responsibility can relieve you of a difficult task at a time when you are least equipped to do it.

Even two-to-three-year-olds can understand something of the facts they are given. Many have buried a turtle or seen a dead bird. The adult can relate to their experience if he knows of it. But even if they don't grasp what you are saying now, they know you will answer their questions, and as they comprehend more they can refer back to these talks.

Frequently grief is disguised in strange ways. Christine was mean to everyone at nursery school after her father died. She fought on every occasion, seeming to want to control the other children by her bossiness. Her inability to control the situation of loss—to turn it around and make it not have happened—made her want to control everything else. Her nursery school teacher said, "One of these days when Chris can talk about how bad she feels, some of this argumentative behavior will subside." Indeed, often children act mad as well as bossy. Sometimes they *are* mad because anything painful can inspire anger.

In mourning, some children regress. The last step taken in development is the first to go. If they recently toilet-trained, they may start soiling. If they just started nursery school, they may cling and clutch. Baby talk may recur. Sometimes silliness is observed. One family thought its five-year-old was unfeeling because he clowned at the funeral of his grandmother. "I was trying to make everyone happy," he said. "They all looked so sad."

ALLAYING ANXIETY

Sometimes after a loss children become preoccupied with illness and dying. This is not morbidity but genuine concern. It is one of the reasons I stress honesty in giving the facts.

You (or the person delegated to do this) cannot begin to help any child cope with his anxieties if he hasn't been told the truth. If you see anxiety about minor illnesses and small separations, talk to the worry behind it.

"What do you think will happen?"

"Mary says everybody dies. Will I?"

"No, you are not going to die. This happens when people are much older."

"Will Grandpa die?"

"Someday, but not now."

He may confound you with knowledge about a young person's death. "How come Johnny died?" he asks. Here you weave both comfort and fact into your answer.

"That was an accident. It doesn't happen very often. He had a special sickness."

"Did he get a cold?"

"No, it did not come from a cold or chicken pox. Your sickness is not the same. Johnny had a bad kind that didn't get better. Your sickness gets better."

"Are you sick?"

"No. I will be with you for a long time."

It may seem contradictory to you to tell your child that death comes only to older people. After all, that is not strictly true—young people do die. However, a young child relates the death of a young person to himself, and he has no way of knowing that this is a rare occurrence and not the normal course of things.

You will see children play games sometimes or talk among themselves (often wildly inaccurately despite your efforts to deliver the facts). Don't interfere at the time. Such talk is a way of working things out. Your honesty when they bring questions to you will enable them to see you as a reference point and to come back to you as their comprehension grows.

Growing up implies an ability to see things realistically. Your aim, as my recommendations make clear, is to allow this growing up to occur.

For the most part, children's grief over death (and much of our own) is like the feelings that surround separation. Since no one knows at what age children actually comprehend what death means, it is largely to these feelings that you direct your attention.

"I hate it because it's for always," said six-year-old Susan about the loss of her grandfather.

"When is Grandpa coming back?" asked her sister, age four.

In the first statement there is despair at the finality of death; in the second, the desire for reversibility. Your response is that you know they miss him. It is hard. This reaches to their sorrow about separation. Your understanding is comforting, even though it doesn't alter the facts.

RELIEVING GUILT

The younger the child, the fuzzier his time concept. But as he grows and recognizes the separation as permanent, he comes to deal with it in his own way. What you do is serve as a fact reminder and feeling comforter.

You may have to make clear to him that his wishes did not make this sad thing happen. The child under five is given to the kind of magical thinking that assumes that thoughts are as powerful as actions.

"No, cousin Harriet did not die because you were angry at her. Thoughts can't make things happen."

Children tend to blame themselves for such painful events as hospitalization, divorce, illness, and death.

"If only I'd worn my boots like Daddy told me to," sobbed Martin when hearing of his father's surgery.

Cause and effect are unclear to young children. Children project themselves into conflicts as they try to understand why things happen.

"I should have been nicer to Edna."

"Robby got sick because I punched him."

This kind of thinking is at the heart of our own superstitions. We don't believe black cats are bad luck, but we'll cross the street to avoid one—just in case.

When young children struggle with causation, they tend to personalize. You may have to tell them again and again that one event had nothing to do with another. By being realistic you help their anxiety significantly.

Families must deal with death in accordance with their own customs, religious beliefs, and preferences. My own view is that a child under five is better off excluded from the funeral service. It may be too much for him to take in. Talking with him afterward may be more to the point. If you decide to take the young child to the service because you do not wish to exclude him from the family's solidarity, be sure to prepare him for what he will hear and allow him to ask questions afterward. If he questions what the clergyman says, you can express your own agreement or disagreement. It is all right to say that nobody knows for sure. I don't think viewing the body helps the very young understand death better; in fact, it is more than the young intellect can assimilate.

It is better for the family to remain in the same house after a death than to make a precipitous move. In this way, the child doesn't lose everything—place as well as person. If you must move, talk about it and be prepared for the "looking back" feelings that such a move will bring.

If a young child witnesses some particular horror surrounding a death, such as a brutal accident or murder, it is important to seek professional help. Talking to a social worker from a children's agency or to a child psychiatrist or psychologist will give the child a chance to express his emotions and to deal with them realistically. This is really a mental health measure which can help to prevent future emotional problems.

Assuring the young child that he is still safe and that he

will still be cared for is the most crucial aspect to handling death. His concern for self is central in the first five years. Your task is to help him feel protected in the face of frightening loss.

X
Hospitalization

Some philosopher has been quoted as saying that he couldn't be a philosopher when his toe hurt. Right. None of us is very philosophical about pain, particularly our own. The world looks very lopsided when we hurt, and going into a hospital hurts, whether we are in pain or not. Anticipating injury makes us anxious even if the aim is to make us feel better.

For the child under five, this is especially true. Hospitalization is a frightening experience. There is the strangeness of a new place to contend with. There is the separation from the people he counts on most. The young patient may be in pain from the illness or injury which causes him to be hospitalized. What further complicates the situation is that his concerns about himself often bear little relation to the severity of the situation. An earache that subsides with a shot is hardly in the same category as an ear problem that requires surgery. A broken leg in a cast is not an amputation. The child himself is often not able to make these distinctions. Thesi Bergman, in her book *Children in the Hospital* (Hallmark Press, 1965), makes this important point. The loss of a tooth to a very young child may be the same as the loss of an eye. This accounts for the overreaction young children may have to very minor procedures.

TELL HIM THE TRUTH

Your first job then when he is facing hospitalization will be to make these distinctions for him. This will necessitate your knowing the facts, not merely what his hospital stay will mean in terms of his future health, but also what specifically is going to happen. He needs to be told why he is going to the hospital and what will be done to him when he gets there.

Getting the facts is not always easy. Doctors and nurses are busy people; they are bombarded daily with trauma and tragedy. Thus the request for specific information, particularly information of a routine sort, may seem unimportant and time-wasting to them. But the child under five does not really understand these distinctions, and it is important that you get as much specific information as you can about what is going to happen to him. In effect, you become a liaison between the staff and your child. Of course, it may not be fun to be placed in that position, but it helps him and that is the issue.

Your own feelings of helplessness and worry will need to be dealt with if you are to serve your child. Getting the facts straight from the doctor helps you too.

The steps involved in preparing a child for hospitalization are the same as those for separation: tell him what is coming, help him cope as it happens, and hear him out afterward. Responding to the questions that arise requires that you know the answers.

The child under three may have difficulty understanding what will be done, but tell him anyhow. Unrolling the worry about the event will come later. Different procedures produce different anxieties, and you will have to modify your verbal preparation according to the situation that you face. If the hospital stay is elective, try to arrange a dry run ahead of time. Take him for a visit to the building. Show him what his hospital room will look like, let him meet at least some of the people who will be handling him, and tell him what will happen next. All these steps help to reduce unnecessary worry.

STAY NEARBY

Whenever possible, try to stay with him. After six months of age the child is very much aware of your absence. Some hospitals have built adjoining rooms so that mothers can sleep in and be near their children. If your hospital does not have these modern rooming facilities, see if a cot can be put in his room. If not, curl up on a blanket on the floor. All young children benefit from having their mothers there, but for the child under three this especially important. Separation in addition to pain is very hard for him to handle. If you cannot possibly be there, see if someone he knows and cares about can be near.

The young child's ability to judge time is poor, and even a brief illness can seem endless to him. You may be embarrassed if your child carries on, but try not to worry about it too much. Many of those who carry on are those who master the misery sooner. Since adaptation abilities vary in children, it is hard to predict what your child's reaction will be. However, the basic differences in children's reactions are those of degree, not kind. One of the most difficult things very young children face in the hospital is the loss of their own growing independence. The hospital makes them babies again, passively cared for; it helps if they can gripe about it, just as the chairman of the board might do under similar circumstances.

For emergency hospitalization there will not be time for preparation, but be sure to talk over your child's feelings about what happened after he's home. Children tend to think hospitalization is some kind of punishment for wrongdoing. If you listen to his play after he returns home, you may get some clues as to what he erroneously links together.

RELIEVE HIS FEARS

Chuck, age four, in for a tonsillectomy, came out of surgery holding his genitals.

"I wasn't operated on," he said, pointing to his penis. "See?" This response came despite excellent preparation about what would be happening.

The worry about body damage seems to focus on the genitals after the toddler stage. As in sex education, if you ask him first what he thinks happened (his fantasies often reveal his worries), you will be better able to educate to the point of his concerns.

Since children are steadily moving through various phases of development, you can expect that whenever something upsets their inner balance (fairly unsteady anyhow), time will be required to right it.

Hospitalization is especially hard for the two-to-three-year-old. Tell him what is coming approximately two days ahead of the event. There are records as well as books available on the subject, and their neutrality can assist you in establishing your own self-control. When the big day comes, let him take along a favorite toy.

For the three-to-five year old, give about a week's preparation. Once again, as with all children, it is telling the facts that is important. Be brief and to the point. Try not to get into involved explanations. For example, regarding a tonsillectomy:

"You have to go to the hospital."

"The doctor is going to make you well."

"Yes, you will get a shot. But he will tell you when he is going to give it."

"Yes, it will hurt. He is going to cut out a piece of your tonsils which you don't need. But you will be asleep when he does it."

"When you wake up it will be over and the nurse will give you medicine to stop the hurting."

Don't avoid the hurting part. Most of us were told that we would be given a treat when we went into the hospital. Our parents didn't want us to know that any pain was involved.

Reactions will vary.

"I won't go!" said Larry. Talk revealed that he was afraid. "Who wouldn't be?" said his mother. "But you have to go anyhow."

Carol was serene. "I'm a big girl. It's okay." Afterward she cried. "If that's a hospital, I don't like it!"

Tommy covered his ears and started to sing loudly and gaily.

PREPARE HIM FOR THE UNEXPECTED

Even if you are as honest as you can be about what is to happen, you will still have to prepare him for the unexpected. Sometimes a child will see things in a way you couldn't have predicted. You may have to answer questions about the other children who are ill. Also, there are always unplanned things —the unexpected change of nurse, the intravenous shot which you did not anticipate.

"Sometimes something will happen that I don't know about now, but you can tell me about it if it happens."

The whole point of preparation is activity—both on your part and on your child's part. The emphasis is on reality— who, what, when, where, and why. Allow for negative feelings, but don't let him wallow in them. After a time, be firm. "But that's how it has to be." Always tell him when you are leaving. Always tell him when you will be back. If other family duties prevent your visiting as often as you would like or as often as you promised, be sure to call, even though you may feel hurt at the reception your thoughtfulness receives. Send a small gift. Keep in touch. Comfort comes in all sizes, and it's not spoiling to indulge a bit with extra treats. Hurts deserve some compensation.

You may hear from the nurses that your child behaves

beautifully until you appear. He may start crying the minute he sees you. This is normal. He is only letting down after being good for strangers. It is a compliment, for he is safe in blaming his parents. They love him. He says, in effect, "How could you let them do this to me?"

Some hospitals employ staff members who devote themselves to helping children through the difficult emotional ordeal of hospitalization. These people are aware that a child may be tearful or fearful when he sees what is happening to other children. They see to it that a quiet place is provided for the child; they are available for explanation and calming down. No child under three can really understand why someone other than his mother should be caring for him. Thus the staff people who most often do this work (nurses, social workers, and child-care workers) often find themselves with angry patients. It takes a long time for trust to develop. With chronic patients, this is possible; with short-term patients, using mothers is often the best way. Here relaxed visiting rules help. When the needs of the whole child are understood, parents are not seen as interlopers.

Parents often learn a great deal about handling their children by observing the child-care staff in the hospital. Frequently such workers help the parents after the child leaves the hospital, not merely with the physical matters which need attention but also with the feelings involved. It is tacitly understood that the parents are important in what will follow at home.

WHEN HE COMES HOME

Talk and more talk should be encouraged upon your child's return. It can take the form of play in which he works his feelings over. Sometimes he will be more direct. We all have a compulsion to relive something which is painful. It is a little like a splinter that must work its way to the surface. When the officer gave you a ticket for going thirty-seven in a thirty-five-mile zone you were properly meek. Then on the way home the dialogue with yourself began. You talked to yourself, you complained about the unfairness, and later you thought of the smart rejoinders you might have made.

A child's way of undoing something painful often takes the form of turning incidents around. If allowed to (at the hospital or at home), he now plays doctor. He gives shots to his dolls or stuffed toys. He yells orders and is very bossy and often mean (that's how it felt to him). This time he is the active perpetrator. Don't try to stop the play (as long as it's done to inanimate objects and not to children or animals). If he tries to operate on a sibling, tell him he can't. He can only play the game with toys. People have feelings.

"I have feelings," yelled Clyde, five. "The doctor hurt me!"

"That was to get you better."

"I didn't like it."

"Of course you didn't. He had to hurt you and that's no fun."

His anger is a healthy sign. He's working out an old grudge even as you do when you talk to yourself after something unpleasant. After a while the hurt loses its sting, and working it over and over helps to get rid of it for good.

You may see other signs of upset. Regression is one. Whining, thumbsucking, even wetting or soiling may occur. Encourage your child to put his complaints into words. Tell him you think he's having accidents because he's upset about what happened. If he doesn't respond to talk, make up a doctor or nurse game which includes his experiences. Generally he will become enthusiastic about this game, and as he becomes active, the more passive infantilisms will disappear. You can hold the line on his cleaning up his messes, but do make the connection for him.

By voicing his sadness, anger, or fear, or whatever emotion he appears to be contending with, you give him power to understand himself. So maturity is aided.

Although hospitalization can be traumatic for a child, it can aid growth—it can help cement the close relationship between parent and child as they work out hard things together. We have learned, in all these painful areas of real-life problems, that it is not what happened that really counts. It is how the person met and dealt with the problem that makes the difference.

XI
Divorce

"Who do I belong to?" asked Tommy, four, after he was told his parents were getting divorced. His first concern was for himself. His clear statement of anxiety testifies to the preschooler's understanding that he can't make it on his own and that someone has to take responsibility for him.

THE LOYALTY CONFLICT

For the young child, divorce marks a change which affects his life in a very unique way. His affections—or disaffections, as the case may be—are split and he is not, as in the case of death, part of a group which is left to mourn together. The comfort of unity in grief is denied him. As he feels affection for one parent, a loyalty conflict ensues about the other. Of course, if one parent has been openly brutal, this conflict is lessened, since presumably the more appropriate parent takes command and in effect rescues him. Even then the child may feel an attachment, unrealistic though it may seem to the observer. Most divorces, however, are not so clear cut. Marriages may flounder on adult incompatibilities of a subtler sort, and these may be unknown to the young child.

He loves both his parents, and he does not see them realistically with lives and interests of their own. The divorce comes as a blow to him, despite the fact that he may have witnessed violent arguments and been worried by outbursts of anger and periods of separation. After all, he is the result of this parental union, and he is tied to the issue of divorce in the same way he was tied to the marriage. His parents may get a divorce, but he cannot. He continues to belong to them even if they no longer belong to each other.

In this age of divorce some of my language may seem antiquated. Do we "belong to each other" any more? Is there not now more of a stress on individual fulfillment? Are there not mothers who do not wish to marry? I cannot argue these issues because it is hard to see, in the middle of the muddle, exactly what is happening to the American family. There are reports which show that divorce is good for children, since they suffer when there is conflict in the home. Staying together has proved a barren journey for many who tried. There are other reports which show that divorce has aftereffects, not always envisaged by those who hoped it would solve problems. No doubt some couples are happier for having divorced, and some are not. The important point is that divorce is more common now than it ever was, and the need to help children cope with it is, therefore, greater than ever before.

It may not be possible for the principals of the divorce to think clearly about their children's needs in the face of rancor and bitterness. Everything that happened earlier in the marriage exerts an influence. Past divisiveness will have an effect on money and custody arrangements. Some couples attempt counseling first, and this is certainly worth a try. Sometimes compromises are reached which restore a balance for a while. Even if the union is ultimately broken, the talking ahead of time gives parents a chance to figure out the best way to talk to their children about the divorce. Much will depend on whatever good feelings remain. Dr. J. Louise Despert, in her book *Children of Divorce* (Doubleday, 1963), says that couples who cannot make a success of marriage can make one of their divorce. The issue, she claims, is caring enough for the children to see their needs as top priorities. It can be a double burden for the partners involved; for while they are struggling to settle their own lives (amid feelings of anger, hurt, revenge, resignation, or whatever), they are still responsible for dealing with the future as well as the feelings of their children.

The temptation to use the child as a weapon in the battle is great on the part of both antagonists. It takes some effort to resist this very human impulse.

"WHAT WILL HAPPEN TO ME?"

The main issue for the child is how this new arrangement will affect his life. Until he is older he does not consider how it affects yours.

So you tell him, "We are separating and are not going to live together. No, it's not your fault. Mommy and Daddy don't get along and think it better if we live apart."

His fear that he will be abandoned because he doesn't get along with the absent parent may or may not be voiced. Talk about this anyhow.

"Daddy is still your Daddy and he loves you. He is going to come visit on Tuesday and Sunday."

This type of explanation will suffice. Children do not need to know all the details which led to the divorce. Their primary concern is what will happen to them, not what happened between you.

Anger toward either or both parents may be expressed. Try to allow it. When loyalty conflicts surface, they do less damage. You know what he is coping with and are then in a position to help him clarify his feelings.

"I can see you are mad at me. That's okay. It's a hard time for you."

He may see you in tears or overhear you in an angry

outburst. You can acknowledge what your feelings are, but still you must reassure him.

"We are still your Mommy and Daddy even if we don't live together any more."

He needs to know that his needs will be met.

"You will live with me. Daddy will visit. Both of us care for you."

"But I want to live together!" he storms. You acknowledge his wish but tell him it can't be. Honesty helps him over the long haul.

Often children are the most difficult to handle just when the parent or parents desperately need peace and quiet. The child is likely to blame the parent he is left with, since that's the one who is handy. In most cases this is the mother. She finds herself trying to maintain a home at the same time that her child accuses her of destroying his.

Mothers who are left to raise children by themselves feel the inequity of divorce. They are the rearers and the daily discipliners and therefore the ones who get the brunt of their children's mixed feelings.

"It's your fault!" a child may say openly. "If you'd been nice to Daddy, this wouldn't have happened!"

A child sometimes glorifies an absent parent. The parent who is away in turn may encourage this by becoming a "treat" person for the few hours spent with the child. This is a disservice to the child; it is self-serving rather than helpful. Counseling (with the aim of helping the child cope with a problem of considerable magnitude in his life) may prove useful to either or both parents when the divorce is definite. Talking it over with a counselor who understands what a divorce means to a child can help the parent who bears the major caretaking job.

One parent cannot be both mother and father to the child, despite the wish to make up for his loss. Talking about the situation with your child puts it in a context. There are still a mother and a father, even though the living situation is different. Even if the other parent is absent permanently, allow the child to talk about it, and tell him the facts so that he doesn't feel someone important to him has dropped into a void. This helps mitigate his feeling of loss. Even though the message is painful for him, don't sidestep it. Don't make the mistake of thinking, "Out of sight, out of mind." He is churning things over, and you keep in touch when you communicate. Talking about loss doesn't restore the past, but neither does it bury it an unrealistic way. Talk helps the child to master a trauma. Despite the pain of divorce, children can cope well when given facts and help with their feelings.

OUTSIDE HELP

Groups which encourage the sharing of common experiences may prove useful. One of these, Parents Without Partners, has chapters in most cities. The Child Study Association of America, 50 Madison Avenue, New York, New York 10010, has pamphlets on the subject of divorce and a guide as to where and when these groups meet. If there isn't a group in your city, you can form one. Activity in your own behalf can help your feeling of helplessness too. Acting on the reality of the separation and coping with the real changes it makes in your life helps your child more than behavior which supports the notion that you can be all things to him. The wish on your part to repair the damage is real. It can be done best by acknowledging the break and dealing with the feelings that attend it.

It is not easy to help your child when you yourself are coping with such a difficult experience. Unlike death, divorce may bring feelings of humiliation and diminished self-worth. The task of helping your child in the midst of these feelings can seem overwhelming, and it is important for you to have some support and relief at this time. Don't feel you have to stay home all the time to compensate for your spouse's absence.

ALLOW FOR A PERIOD OF ADJUSTMENT

Remarriage may seem the answer. You may feel that your new spouse will be a father or mother again to your child. Parents, however, are not so easily substitutable for the child. It is his father (or mother) you are replacing, and he needs time to adjust to the separation. It is better to wait a bit before remarrying. Try to allow for a period of adjustment, in which you and the child get used to living alone. It can be a useful time for talking, for feeling, for expressing the miseries. When some of this is behind both of you emotionally, the child can move into a greater acceptance of what your next step will be. There will still be adjustments, but the first tension will have lessened. It takes a long time for children to accept parents as people with lives of their own. The breather interval helps the process and makes the next step smoother.

If you find you have to go to work, try to give your child some time to prepare for your absence. Otherwise he may feel like he lost both parents simultaneously—one by divorce and the other by absence. See if you can arrange a divorce settlement that allows you to be home for a while before you leave your child with someone else. If this is not possible, do your best to find the right person to take care of your child. Have the housekeeper or sitter spend some time with you and your child before you leave (a week or a month, whatever you can arrange), and prepare to do a lot of listening to the feelings your child will verbalize about the changes in his life. Ideally, you should stay home for a few months—even a year—before returning to work. This is rarely feasible financially, however, and much can be accomplished in a few weeks of explaining and contact with a new caretaker. Once again, the central point is getting your child to accept the realities of the situation. Again, it is your acknowledgment and verbalization of the child's feelings that helps him to accept the facts.

THE FATHER'S ROLE

A number of excellent books have been written about the father's role in divorce. One such book, *Parents Without Partners: A Guide for Divorced, Widowed, or Separated Parents* (E. P. Dutton, 1961), by James and Janet Egleson, is no longer in print but it is still available in public libraries. It sums up the child's need for the father in a most useful way. The Eglesons underscore the following advice for the father, which I have paraphrased:

Don't abdicate (even if you're mad at her). Children need you more than ever. Extra gifts are not necessary. Informal visiting (which recognizes the need for contact but which does not overplay the reparative wish) is best. Watching TV together is as good as going to a football game. Playing games is another way to have fun together. Keep promises about visits. If you must cancel out, tell the children. Write letters and telephone when you must be away.

On the practical side, the Eglesons recommend that visits with the children be kept separate from business visits with the mother and that arrangements about the children be made only during these latter visits. In this way not only are the children left out of what may be an acrimonious exchange, but they receive their father's full attention when they are with him. This last point is very meaningful to the children. It is an affirmation of their position as *his* children. When a father visits his former wife's home, it's a good idea for her to disappear. She can overlook small infractions of her standards as long as they are not excessive. She should try not to pump the children when they return but to listen if they feel like talking.

On important days such as birthdays or graduations both parents can be there. You needn't pretend friendship if you don't feel any, but good manners and an effort at civility will go a long way.

The child appreciates the effort that is being made for him.

A fake friendliness will be recognized, however. If matters are pretty rock-bottom, you can talk about your anger (he perceives it anyhow). Then when you are civil he will recognize your effort as good manners.

DEFECTIONS

The approach is similar with a child who has been deserted by his mother.

"Mommy wasn't able to come for you," said a father in the face of his wife's running off. "She has a pretty bad problem. She wants to come and see you but her problem keeps her away." This is an attempt to soften the blow. While a reason is not an excuse—and the child may tell you so in no uncertain terms—telling him that his mother's defection is not directed against him can be of help until he is able to understand more. You can say, "It makes you angry and sad when Mommy doesn't come."

Smaller defections, such as when a parent says he will come but doesn't, can be just as difficult for the child to bear. Hopes are raised and shattered each time a promise is not kept. The other parent's unreliability, as a fact of the child's life, becomes painfully clear. It takes time for the child to recognize and accept this.

A father who has been awarded custody of his children and who, as family provider, will be away much of the time will need to find a housekeeper to serve in lieu of mother. As with the working mother, careful selection is necessary.

All life is a risk. You may say, "Our marriage didn't work out. I'm sorry about that, but we had you and that is good." Working the sorrow out together can strengthen character too. It should comfort you to know that while the parent who stays with the child gets most of the complaints, in the long run the child knows who put in the effort.

XII
Fathers

Fatherhood changes a man's life. As one father said, "Children make a mess of your life, but somehow you kinda like it."

Most books on child raising emphasize the changes in a mother's life, but it is also true that a new father never comes home to the same life again. It isn't only that babies cry, take up room, and are expensive. Or that your wife seems to be listening with only half an ear, or that the house looks like a madman was at it. It is that your life has been changed instantly and permanently. Someone has moved in for good.

CHANGES OF FATHERHOOD

Luckily, many of the changes are positive ones. You become one of the two most important people in this new person's life. The toddler's leap into your arms when you come home at night can make up for a dozen sleepless nights. "That's my Daddy," from a three-year-old can cancel the choice expletives that came to mind when you stumbled over the tricycle left out on the walk.

In short, there are compensations for the long haul. These are what parents remember fondly in later years. It is the short haul that may be hard, for fathers too are battling against the nature of the child under five. They may be surprised to learn, as are their wives, that the ability to reason comes slowly to little children. Whatever theories about child rearing they held before, they are now faced with the practical reality of balky children who don't always behave as they would like.

For fathers to know that this is the nature of children, and that it is not easy to rear social and considerate human beings from the tyrants toddlers are, is all to the good. It makes for a better understanding of the effort required to produce decent human beings. Some understanding of the irrational nature of the young (see Chapters II, III, and IV on discipline) can cut into the human tendency to blame the wife if the kids are bad. Children have a remarkable ability to stir you up and make you regress from adulthood. Fathers, like mothers, are not immune to the carrying-on of the under-five. You must work together with your wife or the kids will outflank, undermine, and overwhelm you.

The constant demands and messiness of the young child can be wearing on all who try to cope.

"I don't know how she stands it," one father confided. "Working at the office is child's play compared to child's play."

"I don't belong to the TGIF club any more," said another father. "I've joined the Thank God It's Monday group."

"I thought raising children would be a snap," said a third. "Now I think 'I'm okay, you're okay, they're not okay.'"

FATHER'S CONTRIBUTION TO IDENTITY

The issues involved in child care are, therefore, not simple ones. Yet giving no thought to one's role or task as a father is fairly common practice. The role is different from the mother's from the start. Margaret Mead writes, "Children grow toward their fathers." She adds that the child's tie to the mother is a biological one but states, ". . . the child's tie to its father is a social one."* The baby is hatched, as it were, as the mother takes care of him. His sense of identity develops as he is attached to her, separates himself from her, becomes independent of her.

Recognition of whether he or she is a boy or girl begins to develop as he compares similarities and differences. Father as a model contributes to the sexual identity of the boy ("we are similar—you will grow up to be a man"). He contributes to the girl ("We are different but we complement one another"). The appreciation of either sex by the father is important to the developing identity of the child. To be like (for the son), to be liked (for the daughter), contribute to a sense of sexual identity, an important aspect of identity in general. This doesn't mean fathers can't help around the house or that mother is not to pursue her own interests. What you are and what you do are different things and there is more freedom today to complement one another's roles and still remain secure in one's own identity.

Because mother is acquainted with her baby sooner than father, he becomes a person to her very early on. Fathers try to take an interest (some rare few actually do) but as one father put it, "A baby isn't *good* for anything."

"Bring her to me when she's two and can talk."

When the child's ability to think rationally develops, most fathers become really engaged. The pleasure is a mutual one, for the toddler in his growing awareness of everything about him becomes more and more interested in this person who comes and goes.

In some families the father is away frequently; in others he is on the scene almost constantly. Life's demands, career choices and personal interests shape the time a father spends with his children. For most fathers, intermittency is the

*Margaret Mead and Ken Hayman, *Family* (New York: Macmillan Co., 1971), p. 45.

name of the game, for even a job close by requires comings and goings. Father's contribution to the family is usually made in the time left over from his work.

Intermittency has both its advantages and disadvantages. In most homes the father works all day whether the mother works or not. So he has a specialness for his children just by virtue of his not being there so constantly. He can have a freshness of viewpoint, a perspective and a resilience that only being away can bring. Children look forward to their father's return and the reunion may bring a special poignancy. Logjams can be broken up by his coming home; he brings fun and diversion. Or, if he so chooses, in his time at home he can do everything mother does. He can feed, bathe, tell stories. He can help in any way he sees necessary. But by virtue of the fact that he is the one doing it, it becomes special. Often rituals get established, since children like the security of sameness.

"My Daddy reads that book to me. Don't touch it," said one little girl to her sitter.

"Daddy takes me upstairs," said a child to a visiting aunt. "Then Mommy tucks me in." She added, "That's the way we do things around here."

On the disadvantage side, the leaving and the return may bring feelings of dislocation. A father may leave a peaceful household in the morning only to come home to one engaged in a war he knows nothing about.

"I feel as though I've come in in the middle of a movie. It's hard to know what's happened," said one father.

"Shifting gears is rough," said another. "I've had pressure on the job all day. I'd like calm and quiet when I come in. When the kids descend sometimes I feel as though I'd like to hide."

"The kids' interests are so far from the work I'm doing, it takes a leap of the imagination to take them seriously," said a third. "I find it hard to be turned on by bubble gum."

Mothers have the benefits (and hardships) of continuity.

For them the progress and steps of infancy, toddlerdom, and childhood bring advances that they are in touch with daily. Their need is often to break away. "Take me with you!" shouted one mother as her husband left for work.

"I'm stuck here all day," screams another in a famous cartoon caption, "and all you do is work in a nice cool sewer."

REENTRY PROBLEMS

Reentry can bring its own kind of problem for father. If a father has been on business trips a lot, guilt about his being away from the kids may make him a softie.

"What did you bring me?" demands Kathy as soon as the doorbell rings.

There's nothing wrong with an occasional gift, particularly after a long absence, but you shouldn't make presents your means of pacifying your own conscience. If your work demands your being away, prepare the children honestly for your trips, write cards, even call. Keeping in touch is the most important factor, as children learn to accept the way your family has to live. The implication that you are making up for a defection is false and you need not get into that kind of bind.

Because of the intermittent nature of most fathers' contacts with their children, the sharing of ideas between parents is extremely important. Mothers and fathers need to have the same information about what is going on at home. A father has to be involved in whatever concerns the raising of the children, whether it is toilet training, discipline, or study habits. When he and his wife reach agreement on their approach, he can then support it wholeheartedly. Parenthood is really a partnership in the fullest sense, no matter how often father is away, or for how long.

"If your husband doesn't back you up you can forget it," said one wife. It is as important, perhaps even more important than his physical presence. Here quality of time is truly more important than quantity. A man may be home but his only true child may be his briefcase.

A writer of an excellent book about fathers states that the greater the responsibility of the mother for the care of the children, the greater her need for help from her husband because she is deprived of the adult world she knew.* He not only brings the outside world in for the children when he shares things they understand, he brings the grownup world in for her as he confides in her and listens to her about her day. Sometimes fathers are bored with what one father called "the triviality of the world of little kids." It is important to remember that it can feel like this to a mother too. For the parenting job to be done well, emotional support from a husband is worth a thousand lectures.

The role of backup of mother is helpful for all concerned because after a day spent with the unreasonables mother needs this support to preserve her own sanity. The kids need it because it makes their divide-and-conquer monkeyshines less profitable.

Reentry, on the other hand, can easily put a father in the position of heavy.

"I'll tell Daddy on you!" shouts a mother whose patience is exhausted. Two energetic toddlers, being housebound by snow and measles, have reduced her to this weak demonstration of authority.

This practice is actually more common than not. Often mothers rely on fathers for the disciplining they've been threatening all day. In part this happens because mothers are there so constantly that children can easily tune them out. Mothers are also busy people and sometimes the chance for a confrontation disappears under the round of chores. Finally, mothers may be so fed up at the end of a day that they

*Ted Klein, *The Fathers' Book: A Commonsense Guide for Every Man Who Wants To Be a Better Father* (New York: William Morrow, 1968).

say, in effect, "Here, you handle these characters. I've had it!"

PRESENTING A UNITED FRONT

Don't dodge the necessity to take a stand. Fathers play an important role in discipline because it becomes very clear after infancy that little children must be taught to behave better. Don't be afraid to exert your authority. Children need boundaries and feel safer when these are made clear. A child doesn't need a pal in you. He has plenty of those. He needs a father.

It works better when you and she take the time to discuss the children and figure out a strategy that works for both of you as well as for the kids. You double your strength by examining your assets and making them work for you.

One family I know was quite combative about its weaknesses. Mother was angry at father because he couldn't bear to listen to feelings. She felt he was unsympathetic to the children's problems and insensitive to their emotional life. He felt she was a softie who couldn't make anything stick. Each felt wronged and compounded the problem by exaggerating what he or she felt was needed. Father came down more heavily on discipline "to make up for her." Mother listened to complaints more than was necessary because she felt no one else listened.

On the other hand, father *was* sensible about discipline. Mother *was* able to hear. They turned it around. Weakness became asset when she supported his discipline and he encouraged the children to talk to their mother.

The children knew their parents' limitations. (Don't they all?) But they also received a united approach that helped everyone.

Children can create friction between parents. Try not to let them. The goal of viewing the children from a single vantage point takes some doing because you and your spouse

came from different backgrounds and each of you can't help
but respond differently to the various growth stages of your
various offspring. Further, you are of different sexes, bore
different positions in your own families, and had unique
relationships with your own parents. All these play a part in
determining your responses to your children. The effort to
see the other's viewpoint isn't easy but it can make an enormous difference in morale within a family. Whenever a father
makes an effort to respect his wife's feelings about the children it enables her to cope better. And vice versa, for sure.

FINDING YOUR OWN STYLE

Martyrdom, however, isn't good for anybody. A father
doesn't have to be involved in any way that is not natural for
him. Trying to play ball with the kids if you hate sports won't
work, either for you or for them. The real issue is developing
an attitude of support and then finding your own comfortable style of participating. Like diplomacy or motherhood,
fatherhood is the art of the possible. Knowing your own
limitations can help you find compromises that are adequate
for the family and bearable for you.

One father, determined to be an active participant in his
children's life, began to hate Sundays. "He helps me with a
vengeance," said his wife.

It may be better for the whole family to realize you need
relief from your work and the kids as well, and that you need
time for just yourself. The assumption that time with children is a rest for you may not always be true. This father did
better on Sundays by allowing himself a tennis game in the
morning. He then could really enjoy the children in the
afternoon and was able to give his wife a respite. Trading off
nights of sitting is another way to allow some time for each
other's interests. There has to be a balancing of obligations
so that adult needs are met too. You may have to plan ahead
in order to find that balance. Too much sacrifice on your part

can lead to the feeling that you should be rewarded. You may find yourself seeking good behavior from the children as payment for your own good behavior. This robs them and you of genuine independence.

Another father pointed to the condensed nature of his time with his kids. "Six to eight is the arsenic hour in my house. Everyone's hungry. The kids need baths. My wife is exhausted." After thinking it over, his wife changed her schedule. "I now feed the children before he gets home. Since I refuse to cook twice, he may get a twice-heated dinner, but we don't mind because the children are more amiable on full bellies. I also alternate nights for bathing the kids. They're a little dirtier and we're a lot happier."

It doesn't matter how you choose to cope with the abrasive times. Your choice is frequently a matter of custom and habit. But look for the problem areas and see if you can't make some simple changes. Full bellies before discussing *anything* of personal significance is not a bad idea for anyone at any age.

OTHER ROLES OF FATHER

In addition to being an authority figure, a father has a special significance for his children in that he is often able to play with them in ways a mother cannot. His fun is of a different order and sought by children all the more because it is unique. Often it may be whimsical or even downright silly but this can provide a break in the routine that is a release and pleasure for everybody.

"Carry me on your shoulders!" shouts Tom as father walks in.

"Swing me!" begs Susie.

These are happy times for everyone and little need be said about them. Mother sometimes cautions against over-stimulating the children before bedtime and here compromises can be reached if the children are slow to settle in after too much physical play. For a father who enjoys sports the time will come when his children can share them with him. If you find that your children don't share your interests, try not to press them. Recreation pleasures vary and your children have a right to their preferences, as do you.

FATHER AS SYMBOL

Sometimes a father becomes aware that he stirs feelings in his children that he did little realistically to inspire. These come by and large from the child's fundamental immaturity and his overriding need for protection. He will invent qualities in his father as his need for these is demonstrated. The qualities often change as his needs change.

"My Daddy can lick your Daddy," he shouts out of weakness and feelings of powerlessness.

"Daddy will fix it," he consoles himself when he breaks a toy.

"I want to marry my Daddy," says the little girl in her burgeoning femininity.

He can be seen as protector, authority figure, love object. He can be judge, policeman, caretaker. He can be ogre or helper, hated or admired. It helps for a father to know that he didn't do anything to account for these changeable, sometimes contradictory, and often intense feelings. These come out of the magical thinking of childhood.

Evidence of this appears with equal frequency in children whose fathers are permanently absent—through death, desertion, or divorce. These children too have strong feelings about their fathers, seen or unseen, remembered or not. These feelings may represent myth, fact or fancy as the child develops. In such situations a mother may find that having pictures of father about, talking about him or making some attempt at a link to him can help, for recognizing the importance of the symbol of father contributes to a child's identity. Often in these circumstances a child chooses someone else who is close by to serve as a father figure. He will latch onto a neighbor, a friend, or an uncle, chosen on his own to meet his changing requirements. He may never verbalize his feelings or even understand them clearly but it's good to know that the meaning of father need not be lost to him because his actual father is gone.

FATHER AS PERSON

Of greater importance than the symbolic meaning of father in a child's life is a father's realistic relationship with his children. Even the very young child relates largely to his parents on the basis of what they do for and with him. Function is the key word here. Children have attachments to both of their parents, and they respond to them in general in terms of how they are cared for. Children are concerned primarily with their own needs, and they view parental care in terms of how these needs are met. Here a father's realistic relationships with his children reflect his attitudes and qualities as a person. These vary from person to person, so what a father can be to a child will differ from one family to another. Even in families where the father is gone, and another man serves as father figure, the qualities of the person are what count.

Fathers also have an important role to play in the case of emergencies. Sometimes it is necessary for mother to be away —whether for her own hospitalization or to care for someone else in the family. Her work may require her to be out of town for a short time. If father has not been too active in the care of the children before this time, the burden of primary care will tilt suddenly in his direction. He may feel overwhelmed at first, especially if no other help is available. The children need to be fed, bathed, disciplined, and comforted. Comfort in particular may be necessary because they miss their mother. Following her routine as closely as possible will help them adjust to the change.

This is a good time to overlook some things that need doing in the house. If you're a tidy soul, your wife will appreciate the vacuuming and cleaning you do, but more than anything else she will appreciate your attention to the needs of the children. This is the time for shortcuts. TV dinners, peanut butter and jelly sandwiches, paper plates, and drip-dry clothes are fine. When friends invite you for a nice hot meal you may find that it's not as enjoyable a prospect as you thought. You have to get the children there. You have to get them home. Toilet training and other more recently acquired skills may be shaky and you may question the effort involved. If it's easier not to go, stay home. If well-meaning friends want to help, let them bring a hot dish in.

The children may be more demanding and more difficult when mother is away. Secure children often let the parent at home—you—have it, much as they let mother have it when you are gone. The reverse may also occur, however. Children enjoy being with one parent, and a camaraderie develops in meeting a tough situation together. This can make your relationship with your children stronger.

Talk about whatever is wrong in simple terms. Emphasize the positive elements in the situation if you can, and count the days she'll be away. If the children are asleep when she comes home, wake them. For children as well as adults, being an active participant makes things easier to master.

Successful fathering, like successful mothering, puts you out of business. One father said, "I decided a long time ago that you can catch a fish for a child or you can give him a line." If you've determined to do the latter, your child will be on his way to an independence that serves him well.

The satisfactions that come to you as you watch your children's progress are intensely personal ones. These are not derived from the marketplace for father as a father is not defined by his children in terms of his success in the outside world. This is a comforting thought in these days of rapid change and social dislocation. Your family can reflect something of your own spirit, your own doing. Fathers can take pleasure in the power they have to forge a bond of identity with future generations.

XIII
Summing Up

If motherhood is fulfillment, as the books say, it is also ordeal. No matter how much preparation a mother has given to it, she can never be truly experienced before she experiences the experience. When the new baby comes home and uncertainties arise, a mother finds that even though she may not know how to do it, she does it because she has to. Doing the mothering is what makes her a mother. But the process of caring for a child causes other changes in her life that she doesn't anticipate. And some of them are not so easy to take.

Freedom, for one thing, is curtailed—not a little, but a lot. Unless a mother makes advance arrangements for her child to be cared for when she is away, she is totally and absolutely stuck in the home. This is an enormous change for a person who has grown up with a lot of liberty.

For another thing, the newcomer may not bring satisfaction immediately. Some parents enjoy infancy at once, but everyone misses the chance to exchange experiences with a person of some intelligence. This intelligence takes time to develop, and even as it slowly emerges from this tiny cocoon of a baby, it is not the same for you as a peer exchange of equals.

Before motherhood, you were able to exert control over

many things in your life. You could change jobs, take a course, or move away. You may have felt competent in the work you had been trained to do. There is great pleasure in knowing that you are good at something and that the job you are doing is superior. But when the new baby arrives, you are a novice and you may yearn for a return to the familiarity of a work routine. Your equilibrium is upset. The feeling of uncertainty can be painful. "It's like being put into the Olympics after one skiing lesson," said one mother of a newborn.

The first year of a baby's life brings its own normal impasses. The baby has no words to explain and a mother finds herself guessing much of the time. There are those days when she guesses right and he responds; there is the satisfaction that she fixed things and made them right for him. Then there are the days when he is not satisfied no matter what she tries. Those are the times when a mother feels out of phase with her child and begins to wonder about what kind of mother she is. "When nothing works, I feel like a babysitter —sitting for a baby who wants his mother!" said one woman. Although a mother eventually learns to recognize the hungry cry, the tired cry, or the sick cry, often there is the "Maybe it's this but then maybe it's that" cry. She cringes when neighbors give her pat advice which implies that she doesn't know what she's doing. This hurts, especially on days when she may privately agree with them.

There is discord and conflict in child rearing, as well as pleasure. Not everything works smoothly, for despite your efforts children go through normal negative phases. They are limited in their understanding of adult life and they misperceive what you are doing in accordance with their own extremely narrow point of view. What for you may be objective fact (for example, you have to visit your mother in the hospital) is for your child subjective pain. He wants you and can't comprehend that you have demands and loyalties elsewhere. So conflict is a fact of life. You can accept this better when you realize what a far distance the infant has to travel. In the beginning his world fits him. Slowly he must fit into the world. From wanting what he wants when he wants it, he has to learn to wait for what he wants and cope with disappointments along the way. From no frustration tolerance, he has to slowly build such tolerance. From thinking only of his own welfare he has to learn to consider others. He must move from messing to cleanliness, from cruelty to kindness, from barbarism to civilization—and all this takes time. Development also takes a lot out of parents, because they are the ones who help make these more mature responses happen. Conflicts arise because the child's early wishes and your aims are often different.

There is further conflict because a mother is always doing two things at once. Whether it's cooking, talking on the phone, writing a book, or playing the piano, she has one eye on her child's activity and the other on the task at hand. It's two full-time jobs.

You may feel I exaggerate when I point to the ordeal side of parenthood. If so, it is because most of the literature on the subject neglects this, thereby adding unnecessary guilt to the realistic acceptance of normal problems in a child's development. It is important to admit the less happy side of child rearing so that you too can be in touch with your feelings and therefore handle them better. What is good for baby in the development of honest feelings is good for Mommy and Daddy too. Parents also have the right to feel two ways about things. They need not act these mixed feelings out. They too can use words. Greater mastery of self comes when we recognize the bad as well as the good feelings in ourselves. We are then less inclined to take them out on our children just because they are there and they are smaller.

Somehow many think it's easy to be a mother. Mothering is seen as an innate instinct which will take care of things without effort or reflection. This may be so in the animal world, although even biologists might argue there, but it is certainly not true of human beings. For there are ways and there are ways of caring for a baby. To help raise a mature person takes more than physiology and more than instinctive response. In the first five years of life a child can come either a long way or a short way. The long way is harder because insight can bring conflict; understanding can bring pain. Mastery of these brings future benefits, but in the present the task is not easy.

The aim of this book is to help your child grow up, not just grow. It is designed to guide him toward a maturity that isn't pretense and to offer suggestions that help him achieve it. If you are being asked to do this hard thing (more difficult for some of you than for others, depending on how your parents raised you), there ought to be greater recognition of your contribution on the part of society in general. Job mobility, urban loneliness, and fragmented family ties rob young mothers of emotional support when they most need it—when their children are young.

The task for mothers is harder in the face of these difficulties, and they need the support of others in their community if good parenting is to happen. If the importance of good parenting is recognized, ways may be developed to help young parents who are so often isolated. Qualified babysitters can be useful in bringing relief; housekeepers can serve as grandmother substitutes. It takes ingenuity to get the help that aids the rearing of young children. But it is important that ways be devised. Parenthood should not be an impossibly strenuous state for mothers and fathers. Parents should be allowed to keep their spontaneity and enjoy their children as they grow.

When you view a territory from a plane, the contours of land, water, and space become visible to the eye. A design emerges. But distance is necessary for this to happen, and distance is not always possible when you care for a young child. As one wit put it, "The trouble with life is that it's so daily." With the constant interaction required of you, you may not be able to see the forest for the trees. This book tries to redress that inevitable short-sightedness and to help you get a handle on how a child develops. Being able to recognize what will happen next can make you more confident. Knowing what to expect from your child (with some suggestions as to how you might cope) can relieve anxiety.

The assumptions underlying the guidelines in this book do not rest solely on our knowledge of child development. The guidelines assume that you want to help develop a more mature child rather than a less mature one. They assume that you want to see your child become independent and master of himself. The issue of his becoming a trusting as well as trusted person is implicit in the suggestions which have been given. The goal is character development in the old-fashioned sense of the term. One may argue what morality is and what it consists of, recognizing that individuals and cultures vary enormously in the tenets they hold. But no culture exists without standards, and you have a right to your own, a right to raise your children to meet your own standards. They will find their own way better if they've been given a clear start by you.

I have emphasized that the decencies have to be taught, that they don't just happen without your explicit expectation and involvement. Later when your child is confronted with important moral choices, he will be able to be his own person and make his own decisions. The "situational morality" that prevails will not find him yielding to every current trend and fad. He will have a stance from which to judge because you gave him one. This is quite a legacy for you to leave behind.

Index

sense Guide for Every Man Who Wants To Be a Better Father, 154
fears, 67–69
in bathroom, 67–68
at death in family, 124–125
at divorce, 143–145
of hospitalization, 136–137
sexual guilt as cause of, 83
fighting, 58–60
food aversions, 54
funerals, effect on child of, 131

Ginott, Haim, 17
Gruenberg, Sidonie Matsner, 95–96
guilt:
about death, 130–132
about sex, 72–73, 74, 83

Hayman, Ken, 151*n*
honesty:
about death, 126–128, 129
about divorce, 143–145
about hospitalization, 134
in sex education, 77–78, 89–90, 95
hospitalization of child, 133–140
under age five, 134, 136
under age three, 134–135, 136, 138
anger in, 138, 139
coming home after, 138–139
description of child's feelings in, 133
honesty about, 134–135
messing after, 139
parent staying nearby during, 135
regression after, 139
relieving fears of, 136–137
as separation, 135

unexpected events during, 137–138
house moving, *see* moving
How New Life Begins, 96

infantile sexuality, 73–74

love, discipline and, 22–23, 27–28
loyalty conflict, after divorce, 141

masturbation, 85–86
Mead, Margaret, 150–151
Meeks, Esther K., 96
messiness, 64–66
after hospitalization, 139
nagging and, 65
in toilet training, 9–11, 12–13, 17, 21
middle child, parallel stories as aid to, 104–105
modesty:
invasions of privacy and, 98–99
as "preventive medicine," 99–100
in public facilities, 96–97
sex education and, 73, 74–76, 77, 79–80, 83, 90, 96–99
motherhood, sainthood myth and, 28–29
mothers:
hospitalization of, 117–118
Oedipus complex and, 81–84
sex education and, 71
working, 120–122, 146
moving:
after death in family, 131
and separation anxieties, 119–120

nagging, 38
eating problems and, 53
about untidiness, 65